From left to right: **Teddy Blanket**
in Peacock (144), Scarlet (140),
Grass (141), Daisy Yellow (142)
and Fuchsia (143) pattern
on page 68
Pernilla Dress in Peacock (144)
pattern on page 102

CONTENTS

INTRODUCTION

In this book you will find Bright Young Things. A collection of fun, vibrant colourful knitwear, featuring multi-colour stripes and fresh, clashing patterns. Mix bright colours with core dark shades for a fabulous combination or be even more bold and clash brights against each other. Bright Young Things indulges our naughty tendencies, inviting you and your children into our playful mismatched world. Features on the items are deliberately varied to celebrate the quirky and the unconventional. Different colours on opposite sleeves, a contrasting back with a conservative front. Dare to stand out and be different.

Bright Young Things completely captures the ethos behind MillaMia. A belief that you can combine a love of knitting with a love of modern contemporary design and quality. As ever our patterns are inspired by the latest fashion trends, our colours are adapted seasonally and our yarn is made from the finest quality, washable Merino wool. And the entire look is influenced by our Scandinavian design heritage.

PUTTING COLOUR AT THE CORE

At MillaMia we pride ourselves on the colour range our yarn is available in, and the depth and intensity of colour we have achieved. The designs in Bright Young Things would not have been possible without these intense, fresh, vivid colours.

As with our other collections, the colours suggested in this book represent our vision, but the beauty of knitting is the ability to personalise the design to suit your child. If you look at our website, www.millamia.com, you will find a 'Colour Tool' that allows you to experiment, 'playing' with different combinations and making your own colour design decisions.

SOMETHING TO KEEP

Hand knitting a garment is a totally different concept to popping into a shop or logging on and buying a ready made item. It is not as instant or even as easy. But in our view that is part of the thrill and satisfaction of knitting something by hand. The time and care invested in the piece add a value to it that money cannot buy. And given the attention and effort that goes into producing a hand knit garment we feel that the finished result should be really high quality and stylish. It should be worth the effort.

That is why we have ensured our yarn is of the best quality, and easy and consistent to knit with. It is forgiving and quick for beginners, yet fine enough to enable our patterns to achieve the best possible shape and stitch definition so as to reward more advanced knitters. Aware of the everyday realities of living with small children however we also know that for an item to become a favourite there are two further essentials – firstly it must be soft for the child to love it – and secondly machine washable for the parents to be happy. Our yarn is both those things.

SOMETHING FOR EVERYONE

People look for different things from their knitting projects. Sometimes you want a quick fix, or a simple, non-challenging knit. Other times you may be looking for a longer term project or a challenge that will have you concentrating or will help you to develop your knitting skills. That is why we've included a broad selection of patterns that range from easy to advanced, some shorter, some longer. Given the inspiration behind this collection and the focus on colour, this book features several patterns that make use of colourwork techniques, and we hope they can inspire you to try this way of knitting if you have never dared before.

And if there is something you really love but feel you don't have the time or the skill to knit, set someone you know that loves knitting in the right direction with the pattern and yarn.

IN A TANGLE?

MillaMia is all about making knitting easy. So if you find yourself in a bit of a tangle and not sure what to do next, or you are a beginner looking for help to get started, log on to our website www.millamia.com and search through the 'Making Knitting Easy' section. There you can get advice, or download tools, post a question for our technical experts, organise a knitting class or indeed find someone who can help knit the item for you.

We check every MillaMia pattern numerous times before we go to print. Despite this occasionally there can be errors in knitting patterns. If you see what you think is an error the best thing is to visit www.millamia.com where any errors that have been spotted will be published under 'Pattern Revisions'. If you cannot find the answer you are looking for, then do send an email or contact us via the website and we will get back to you as soon as possible to help.

Oskar Jumper in Midnight (101), Snow (124), Claret (104), Plum(162), Seaside (161) and Peacock (144) pattern on page 88

BASIC INFORMATION

SKILL LEVELS

Recognising that we are not all expert knitters we have graded each pattern in the book to allow you to gauge whether it is one that you feel confident to try. The grades are as follows:

Beginner: You have just picked up (or refound) knitting needles and are comfortable with the basic concepts of knitting. By reading carefully you can follow a pattern. Items such as scarves and blankets and simple jumpers are ideal for you to start with.

Beginner / Improving: Having knitted a few pieces you are now looking to try new things, for instance colour combinations and features such as pockets. You might surprise yourself by trying some of the simpler colourwork patterns in this book – you will find that they are not as difficult as you may have thought. Bear in mind that most experienced knitters will be happy to help a beginner so you can always ask for help too! Or look at our website for advice and help.

Improving: You have knitted a variety of items such as jumpers, cardigans and accessories in the past, and are comfortable with following patterns. You may have tried your hand at cable knitting and some form of colourwork before.

Experienced: You are comfortable with most knitting techniques. You have preferences and likes and dislikes, although are willing to try something new. You can read patterns quickly and are able to adapt them to your own requirements – for instance if resizing is needed.

YARN – SOME ADVICE

As there can be colour variations between dye lots when yarn is produced, we suggest that you buy all the yarn required for a project at the same time (with the same dye lot number) to ensure consistency of colour.

The amount of yarn required for each pattern is based on average requirements meaning they are an approximate guide.

The designs in this book have been created specifically with a certain yarn composition in mind. The weight, quality, colours, comfort and finished knit effect of this yarn is ideally suited to these patterns. Substituting for another yarn may produce a garment that is different from the design and images in this book.

For some of the heavier items in this book we have used a technique where we 'use the yarn double'. This simply means using two balls of yarn at once on a thicker needle (in our patterns a 5mm (US 8) needle) to produce a thicker quality to the knitted fabric. An advantage of this technique is that the garment will be quicker to knit up. Make sure you keep your two working balls of yarn spaced separately so that they do not tangle while knitting.

TENSION / GAUGE

A standard tension is given for all the patterns in this book. As the patterns are in different stitch types (e.g. stocking, garter, rib, etc.) this tension may vary between patterns, and so you must check your tension against the recommendation at the start of the pattern. As matching the tension affects the final shape and size of the item you are knitting it can have a significant impact if it is not matched. Ensuring that you are knitting to the correct tension will result in the beautiful shape and lines of the original designs being achieved.

To check your tension we suggest that you knit a square according to the tension note at the start of each pattern (casting on an additional 10 or more stitches to the figure given in the tension note and knitting 5 to 10 more rows than specified in the tension note). You should knit the tension square in the stitch of the pattern (e.g. stocking, garter, rib, etc.).

Once knitted, mark out a 10cm by 10cm / 4in by 4in square using pins and count the number of stitches and rows contained within. If your tension does not quite match the one given try switching to either finer needles (if you have too few stitches in your square) or thicker needles (if you have too many stitches) until you reach the desired tension.

USEFUL RESOURCES

We believe that using quality trims with our knitwear gives the garments a professional finishing touch. Visit your local yarn/ haberdashery shop for these items and MillaMia yarn or visit www.millamia.com to order yarn directly or find local stockists.

SIZES

Alongside the patterns in this book we give measurements for the items – as two children of the same age can have very different measurements, this can be used as a guide when choosing which size to knit. The best way to ensure a good fit is to compare the actual garment measurements given in the pattern with the measurements of an existing garment that fits the child well.

Please note that where a chest measurement is given in the table at the top of each pattern this refers to the total measurement of the garment around the chest. When the cross chest measurement is given graphically in the accompanying diagrams this is half the around chest measurement. Children's clothes are designed with plenty of 'ease', this means that there is not as much shaping or fit to a child's garment as you will find in adult knitwear.

CARE OF YOUR GARMENT

See the ball band of MillaMia Naturally Soft Merino for washing and pressing instructions. Make sure you reshape your garments while they are wet after washing, and dry flat.

LANGUAGE

This book has been written in UK English. However, where possible US terminology has also been included and we have provided a translation of the most common knitting terms that differ between US and UK knitting conventions on page 9. In addition all sizes and measurements are given in both centimetres and inches throughout.

Remember that when a knitting pattern refers to the left and right sides of an item it is referring to the left or right side as worn, rather than as you are looking at it.

READING COLOUR CHARTS

For some of the patterns in this book there are colour charts included. In a colour chart one square represents one stitch and one row. A key shows what each colour in the chart refers to. Remember that when following a knitting chart right side rows (knit when working in stocking stitch) are worked from right to left, and wrong side rows (purl when working in stocking stitch) are worked from left to right. The bottom row of the chart indicates the first row of knitting, and as you work your way up, each row of the chart illustrates the next row of knitting. Repeats are the same for all sizes, however different sizes will often require extra stitches as the repeat will not exactly fit. These stitches are marked by vertical lines showing the start and end of rows.

Niklas Cardigan
in Daisy Yellow (142), Fuchsia (143) and Putty Grey (121)
pattern on page 80

Tobias Hooded Top
in Storm (102) and Seaside (161)
pattern on page 30

ABBREVIATIONS

alt	alternate
approx	approximately
beg	begin(ning)
cont	continue
dec	decrease(ing)
foll	following
g-st	garter stitch
inc	increase(ing)
k or K	knit
k2 tog	knit two stitches together
m1	make one stitch by picking up the loop lying before the next stitch and knitting into back of it
m1p	make one stitch by picking up the loop lying before the next stitch and purling into back of it
mths	months
p or P	purl
p2 tog	purl two stitches together
patt	pattern
psso	pass slipped stitch over
pwise	purlwise
rib2 tog	rib two stitches together according to rib pattern being followed
rem	remain(ing)
rep	repeat(ing)
skpo	slip one, knit one, pass slipped stitch over – one stitch decreased
sl	slip stitch
st(s)	stitch(es)
st st	stocking stitch
tbl	through back of loop
tog	together
yf	yarn forward
yo	yarn over
yon	yarn over needle to make a st
yrn	yarn round needle
y2rn	wrap the yarn two times around needle. On the following row work into each loop separately working tbl into second loop
[]	work instructions within brackets as many times as directed

UK AND US KNITTING TRANSLATIONS

UK	US
Cast off	Bind off
Colour	Color
Grey	Gray
Join	Sew
Moss stitch	Seed stitch
Tension	Gauge
Stocking stitch	Stockinette stitch
Yarn forward	Yarn over
Yarn over needle	Yarn over
Yarn round needle	Yarn over
y2rn	yo2

KNITTING NEEDLE CONVERSION CHART

Metric, mm	US size
2	0
2.25	1
2.5	1
2.75	2
3	2
3.25	3
3.5	4
3.75	5
4	6
4.25	6
4.5	7
5	8
5.5	9
6	10
6.5	10.5
7	10.5
7.5	11
8	11
9	13
10	15

GLAD
SCARF
HELENA
CARDIGAN

From left to right: **Helena Cardigan** in Fuchsia (143), Petal (122) and Grass (141) pattern on page 12, **Glad Scarf** in Fuchsia (143) and Grass (141) pattern on page 18

HELENA CARDIGAN

SKILL LEVEL **Improving**

SIZES / MEASUREMENTS

To fit age	6-12	12-24	24-36	36-48	48-60	mths

ACTUAL GARMENT MEASUREMENTS

Chest	57	60	63	66	69	cm
	22 ½	23 ½	24 ¾	26	27	in
Length to	28	31	34	38	42	cm
shoulder	11	12 ¼	13 ¼	15	16 ½	in
Sleeve	17	19	22	24	28	cm
length	6 ¾	7 ½	8 ¾	9 ½	11	in

MATERIALS

- 2(2:2:3:3) 50g/1 ¾oz balls of MillaMia Naturally Soft Merino in Petal (122) (B).
- Two balls in each of Fuchsia (143) (A) and Grass (141) (C).
- Pair each of 3mm (US 2) and 3.25mm (US 3) knitting needles.
- Circular 3mm (US 2) knitting needle.
- Two buttons approx 21mm/ ⅞in diameter.

TENSION / GAUGE

25 sts and 34 rows to 10cm/4in square over st st using 3.25mm (US 3) needles.

HINTS AND TIPS

A beautiful, wrapover cardigan, that is deliciously, deliberately quirky with contrast pattern and colour pieces. And as there is nothing more complicated than moss (seed) stitch, some shaping and horizontal stripes this makes an accessible piece for the improving knitter to try.

ABBREVIATIONS

See page 9.

SUGGESTED ALTERNATIVE COLOURWAYS

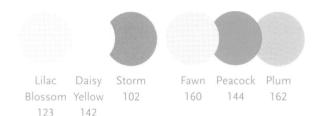

Lilac Blossom 123	Daisy Yellow 142	Storm 102		Fawn 160	Peacock 144	Plum 162

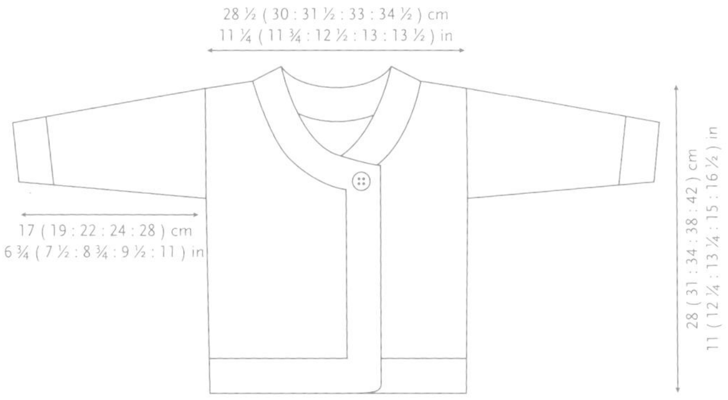

28 ½ (30 : 31 ½ : 33 : 34 ½) cm
11 ¼ (11 ¾ : 12 ½ : 13 : 13 ½) in
17 (19 : 22 : 24 : 28) cm
6 ¾ (7 ½ : 8 ¾ : 9 ½ : 11) in
28 (31 : 34 : 38 : 42) cm
11 (12 ¼ : 13 ¼ : 15 : 16 ½) in

BACK

With 3mm (US 2) needles and A cast on 73(77:81:85:89) sts.
Moss st row K1, [p1, k1] to end.
Rep the last row 17 times more.
Break off A.
Change to 3.25mm (US 3) needles.
Beg with a k row, work in st st and stripes of 8 rows B and
4 rows C until back measures 23(26:29:33:37)cm/
9(10 ¼:11 ¼:13:14 ½)in from cast on edge, ending with a p row.
Shape back neck
Next row K29(30:31:32:33), turn and work on these sts for first
side of neck shaping.
Dec one st at neck edge of next 10 rows. 19(20:21:22:23) sts.
Work 5 rows.
Shape shoulder
Cast off 9(10:10:11:11) sts at beg of next row.
Work 1 row.
Cast off rem 10(10:11:11:12) sts.
With right side facing slip centre 15(17:19:21:23) sts onto a
holder, rejoin yarn to rem sts, k to end.
Dec one st at neck edge of next 10 rows. 19(20:21:22:23) sts.
Work 6 rows.
Shape shoulder
Cast off 9(10:10:11:11) sts at beg of next row.
Work 1 row.
Cast off rem 10(10:11:11:12) sts.

LEFT FRONT

With 3mm (US 2) needles and A cast on 55(59:63:65:67) sts.
Moss st row K1, [p1, k1] to end.
Rep the last row 17 times more.
Change to 3.25mm (US 3) needles.
Break off A.
Next row (right side) With B, k to last 13 sts, join on A,
moss st 13A.

Next row Moss st 13A, using B p to end.
These 2 rows form the st st with moss st border.
Work straight until front measures 16(18:20:23:26)cm/
6 ¼(7:8:9:10 ¼)in from cast on edge, ending with
a wrong side row.
Shape neck
Next row Patt to last 13 sts, leave these sts on a holder.
Next row Cast off 5 sts, patt to end.
Next row Patt to end.
Next row Cast off 4 sts, patt to end.
Next row Patt to end.
Next row Cast off 3 sts, patt to end.
Next row Patt to end.
Next row Cast off 2 sts, patt to end.
Next row Patt to end.
Next row P2 tog, patt to end.
Rep the last 2 rows until 19(20:21:22:23) sts rem.
Cont straight until front measures same as back to shoulder,
ending at armhole edge.
Shape shoulder
Cast off 9(10:10:11:11) sts at beg of next row.
Work 1 row.
Cast off rem 10(10:11:11:12) sts.

RIGHT FRONT

With 3mm (US 2) needles and A cast on 55(59:63:65:67) sts.
Moss st row K1, [p1, k1] to end.
Rep the last row 17 times more.
Change to 3.25mm (US 3) needles.
1st row (right side) Moss st 13A, join on C, k to end.
2nd row With C, p to last 13 sts, moss st 13A.
These 2 rows form the st st with moss st border.
Work straight until front measures 16(18:20:23:26)cm/
6 ¼(7:8:9:10 ¼)in from cast on edge, ending
with a wrong side row.

Shape neck

Next row With A, moss st 13, leave these 13 sts on a holder, then patt to end.

Next row Patt to end.

Next row Cast off 5 sts, patt to end.

Next row Patt to end.

Next row Cast off 4 sts, patt to end.

Next row Patt to end.

Next row Cast off 3 sts, patt to end.

Next row Patt to end.

Next row Cast off 2 sts, patt to end.

Next row Patt to end.

Next row Skpo, patt to end.

Rep the last 2 rows until 19(20:21:22:23) sts rem.

Cont straight until front measures same as back to shoulder, ending at armhole edge.

Shape shoulder

Cast off 9(10:10:11:11) sts at beg of next row.

Work 1 row.

Cast off rem 10(10:11:11:12) sts.

RIGHT SLEEVE

With 3mm (US 2) needles and A cast on 25(27:31:35:37) sts.

Moss st row K1, [p1, k1] to end.

Rep the last row 17 times more.

Break off A.

Join on C.

Change to 3.25mm (US 3) needles.

Beg with a k row, cont in st st.

Work 2 rows.

Inc row K3, m1, k to last 3 sts, m1, k3.

Work 3 rows.

Inc row K3, m1, k to last 3 sts, m1, k3.

Work 1(1:1:1:3) rows.

Rep the last 6(6:6:6:8) rows 5(6:6:8:8) times more and then the inc row 0(0:1:0:1) times again. 49(55:61:71:75) sts.

Cont straight until sleeve measures 17(19:22:24:28)cm/6 ¾ (7 ½:8 ¾:9 ½:11)in from cast on edge, ending with a p row. Cast off.

LEFT SLEEVE

Work as given for right sleeve using B instead of C.

NECKBAND

Join shoulder seams.

With right side facing, using 3mm (US 2) circular needle, slip 13 sts from right front holder onto a needle, using A pick up and k14 sts from cast off sts up right front, 24(27:30:33:36) sts up right front neck, 13 sts down right back neck, k15(17:19:21:23) sts from back neck, pick up and k13 sts up left side of back neck, 24(27:30:33:36) sts down left front neck, 14 sts from cast off sts on left front, moss st across 13 sts on left front holder.

Moss st 7 rows.

1st buttonhole row [K1, p1] 3 times, k2 tog, y2rn, skpo, moss st to last 10 sts, k2 tog, y2rn, skpo, [p1, k1] 3 times.

2nd buttonhole row Moss st to end, working twice into y2rn, working second loop tbl.

Moss st 7 rows.

Cast off in moss st.

MAKE UP

Sew on sleeves. Join side and sleeve seams. Sew on buttons.

GLAD OVERSIZED SCARF

SKILL LEVEL **Beginner**

SIZES / MEASUREMENTS
To fit age   Toddler

ACTUAL MEASUREMENTS
Length   140   cm
                55   in

Width   20   cm
              8   in

MATERIALS
- Three 50g/1 ¾oz balls of MillaMia Naturally Soft Merino in Midnight (101) (M).
- Three balls in contrast Lilac Blossom (123) (C).
- Pair of 3.25mm (US 3) knitting needles.

TENSION / GAUGE
38 sts and 36 rows to 10cm/4in square in single rib patt (k1, p1) slightly stretched using 3.25mm (US 3) needles.

HINTS AND TIPS
A bright and vibrant, oversized striped scarf. Thanks to its single rib construction it lies flat and avoids curling. Large enough that it can easily be borrowed by adults!

ABBREVIATIONS
See page 9.

SUGGESTED ALTERNATIVE COLOURWAYS

Grass   Fuchsia   Peacock   Scarlet   Plum   Claret
141   143   144   140   162   104

TO MAKE

With 3.25mm (US 3) needles and using M, cast on 76 sts.

1st row *K1, p1, rep from * to end.

This row sets the patt for single rib.

Cont in rib for a further 27 rows.

✳✳Next row Switch to C and patt to end.

Work a further 27 rows in patt.

Next row Switch to M and patt to end.

Work a further 27 rows in patt.✳✳✳

Rep from ✳✳ to ✳✳✳ 7 times more.

Next row Switch to C and patt to end.

Work a further 27 rows in patt.

Cast off 76 sts.

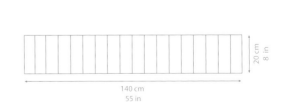

20 cm
8 in

140 cm
55 in

TOBIAS
HOODED TOP
LOTTA
BOLERO

UNO
COWL

From left to right: **Lotta Bolero** in Storm (102) and Fuchsia (143) pattern on page 22, **Tobias Hooded Top** in Storm (102) and Seaside (161) pattern on page 30, **Lotta Bolero** in Scarlet (140) pattern on page 22, **Uno Cowl** in Scarlet (140), Seaside (161) and Midnight (101) pattern on page 28

LOTTA BOLERO

SKILL LEVEL **Improving**

SIZES / MEASUREMENTS

To fit age	2-3	3-4	4-5	years

ACTUAL GARMENT MEASUREMENTS

Chest	62	66	71	cm
	24 ½	26	28	in
Length to	21	23 ½	26	cm
shoulder	8 ¼	9 ¼	10 ¼	in
Sleeve length	22	25	28	cm
with cuffs folded back	8 ¾	10	11	in

MATERIALS

Striped version
- 7(8:9) 50g/1 ¾oz balls of MillaMia Naturally Soft Merino in Storm (102) (M).
- 2 balls in contrast Fuchsia (143) (C).
- Pair each of 4.50mm (US 7) and 5mm (US 8) knitting needles.
- 2 buttons approx 21mm/⅞in diameter.

Plain version
- 8(9:10) 50g/1 ¾ oz balls of MillaMia Naturally Soft Merino in Scarlet (140) (M).
- Pair each of 4.50mm (US 7) and 5mm (US 8) knitting needles.
- 2 buttons approx 21mm/⅞in diameter.

TENSION / GAUGE

18 sts and 24 rows to 10cm/4in square over st st using 5mm (US 8) needles and yarn double.

HINTS AND TIPS

This bolero jacket is completely original and will allow the wearer to stand out from the crowd. Working equally well in either stripes or a single block colour we thought we'd include both alternatives to this pattern. Knitted using the yarn double makes it nice and robust for outerwear. Block the rib of the sleeves slightly stretched for a looser fit on the sleeve.

ABBREVIATIONS

See page 9.

NOTE

Use yarn double **throughout**.

SUGGESTED ALTERNATIVE COLOURWAYS

Striped version

Midnight	Snow
101	124

Moss	Plum
103	162

Plain version

Grass	Midnight
141	101

31 (33 : 35 ½) cm
12 ¼ (13 : 14) in

21 (23 ½ : 26) cm
8 ¼ (9 ¼ : 10 ¼) in

22 (25 : 28) cm
8 ¾ (10 : 11) in

Plain Version

Work as given for striped version, using one colour throughout.

Striped Version

BACK

With 4.50mm (US 7) needles and using M double cast on 58(62:66) sts.
1st row K2, [p2, k2] to end.
2nd row P2, [k2, p2] to end.
Rep the last 2 rows 5 times more.
Change to 5mm (US 8) needles.
Beg with a k row, cont in st st and stripes of 2 rows C and 6 rows M.
Work 8(12:16) rows.
Shape armholes
Next row Cast off 4 sts at beg of next 2 rows. 50(54:58) sts.
Next row K2, skpo, k to last 4 sts, k2 tog, k2.
Next row P to end.
Rep the last 2 rows 4(5:6) times more. 40(42:44) sts.
Work a further 20 rows.
Shape shoulders
Cast off 10(11:11) sts at beg of next 2 rows.
Cast off rem 20(20:22) sts.

LEFT FRONT

With 4.50mm (US 7) needles and using M double cast on 23 sts.
1st row [K2, p2] to last 3 sts, k3.
2nd row P3, [k2, p2] to end.
Rep the last 2 rows 5 times more.
Change to 5mm (US 8) needles.
Beg with a k row, cont in st st and stripes of 2 rows C and 6 rows M.

1st row K to last st, m1, k1.
2nd row P to end.
Rep the last 2 rows 3(5:7) times more. 27(29:31) sts.
Shape armhole
Next row Cast off 4 sts, k to last st, m1, k1. 24(26:28) sts.
Next row P to end.
Next row K2, skpo, k to last st, m1, k1.
Next row P to end.
Rep the last 2 rows 4(5:6) times more. 24(26:28) sts.
Next row K to last st, m1, k1.
Next row P to end.
Rep the last 2 rows 3(2:1) times more. 28(29:30) sts.
Buttonhole row K to last 4 sts, k2 tog, yf, k1, m1, k1.
Next row P to end. 29(30:31) sts.
Shape neck
Next row K10(11:11) sts, turn and work on these sts, leave rem 19(19:20) sts on a holder.
Work 9(11:13) rows.
Shape shoulder
Cast off.

RIGHT FRONT

With 4.50mm (US 7) needles and using M double cast on 23 sts.
1st row K3, [p2, k2] to end.
2nd row [P2, k2] to last 3 sts, p3.
Rep the last 2 rows 5 times more.
Change to 5mm (US 8) needles.
Beg with a k row, cont in st st and stripes of 2 rows C and 6 rows M.
1st row K1, m1, k to end.
2nd row P to end.
Rep the last 2 rows 3(5:7) times more and the 1st row again. 28(30:32) sts.
Shape armhole
Next row Cast off 4 sts, p to end. 24(26:28) sts.
Next row K1, m1, k to last 4 sts, k2 tog, k2.
Next row P to end.

Rep the last 2 rows 4(5:6) times more. 24(26:28) sts.
Next row K1, m1, k to end.
Next row P to end.
Rep the last 2 rows 3(2:1) times more. 28(29:30) sts.
Buttonhole row K1, m1, k1, yf, skpo, k to end.
Next row P to end. 29(30:31) sts.
Shape neck
Next row K19(19:20), leave these sts on a holder, k to end.
10(11:11) sts.
Work 10(12:14) rows.
Shape shoulder
Cast off.

SLEEVES

With 5mm (US 8) needles and using M double cast on
38(42:46) sts.
1st row K2, * p2, k2; rep from * to end.
2nd row P2, * k2, p2; rep from * to end.
Rep the last 2 rows 5 times more and the 1st row again.
Change to 4.50mm (US 7) needles.
Beg with a 1st row, work 12 rows in rib.
Change to 5mm (US 8) needles.
Cont in rib.
Work 2 rows.
Inc row K2, m1, rib to last 2 sts, m1, k2.
Work 3 rows.
Rep the last 4 rows 7(8:9) times more and then the inc row
again. 56(62:68) sts.
Cont in rib until sleeve measures 27(30:33)cm/10 ¾(12:13)in
from cast on edge, ending with a wrong side row.
Shape sleeve top
Cast off 4 sts at beg of next 2 rows. 48(54:60) sts.
Next row K2, skpo, rib to last 4 sts, k2 tog, k2.
Next row Rib to end.
Rep the last 2 rows 4(5:6) times more. 38(42:46) sts.
Cast off 3 sts at beg of next 10 rows.
Cast off.

COLLAR

Join shoulder seams.
With right side facing, using 4.50mm (US 7) needles and M
double, slip 19(19:20) sts from right front on needle, pick up
and k11(13:16) sts up right side of neck, cast on 32(32:34)
sts, pick up and k11(13:16) sts down left side of front neck,
k19(19:20) sts from left front holder. 92(96:106) sts.
Next row K17(17:18), p58(62:70), k17(17:18).
Next row Cast off 17(17:18) sts, k to end.
Next row Cast off 17(17:18) sts, (one st on right hand needle)
k3, [p2, k2] to last 6 sts, p2, k4. 58(62:70) sts.
Next row K2, [p2, k2] 10(11:13) times, p2, turn.
The last 2 rows set rib with 2 sts g-st border.
Next row Rib 30(34:42), turn.
Next 2 rows Rib to last 12 sts, turn.
Next 2 rows Rib to last 8 sts, turn.
Next 2 rows Rib to last 4 sts, turn.
Next row Rib to last 4 sts, p2, k2.
Change to 5mm (US 8) needles.
Cont in rib with 2 sts g-st at each end for a further 10(12:14)
rows.
Work [2 rows C, 2 rows M] twice.
Cast off in rib and M.

FRONT EDGINGS

With right side facing, using 4.50mm (US 7) needles and M
double, pick up and k 42(46:50) sts along each front edge.
K 1 row.
Cast off.

MAKE UP

Join side and sleeve seams reversing on cuff for fold back. Sew
in sleeves. Sew on buttons.

UNO COWL

SKILL LEVEL **Beginner**

SIZES / MEASUREMENTS
To fit age   One size to fit toddler

ACTUAL ITEM MEASUREMENTS
Height   19 ½   cm
               7 ¾   in

Width   24   cm
               9 ½   in

MATERIALS
• One 50g/1 ¾oz ball of MillaMia Naturally Soft Merino
  in each of Scarlet (140) (M), Midnight (101) (A) and
  Seaside (161) (B).
• Pair of 3.25mm (US 3) knitting needles.

TENSION / GAUGE
25 sts and 34 rows to 10cm/4in square over st st using
3.25mm (US 3) needles.

HINTS AND TIPS
Easier to keep on a child than a scarf, the Uno Cowl is a bright,
practical accessory for winter. Block the rib wide to keep the fit
loose and comfortable for the child.

ABBREVIATIONS
See page 9.

SUGGESTED ALTERNATIVE COLOURWAYS

Peacock   Claret   Snow   Fuchsia   Moss   Petal
144   104   124   143   103   122

TO MAKE

With 3.25mm (US 3) needles and M, cast on 122 sts.
1st rib row K5, [p4, k4] to last 5 sts, p5.
Rep the last row for 5cm/2in.
Beg with a k row, cont in st st and stripes of 5 rows A and
3 rows B until work measures approx 14 ½cm/5 ¾in from cast
on edge, ending with 3 rows B.
Cut off A and B.
Join on M.
Next row K to end.
Work 5cm/2in in rib.
Cast off in rib.
Join seam.

24 cm / 9 ½ in

19 ½ cm / 7 ¾ in

TOBIAS HOODED TOP

SKILL LEVEL Improving

SIZES / MEASUREMENTS

To fit age	1-2	2-3	3-4	4-5	years

ACTUAL GARMENT MEASUREMENTS

Chest	60	67	73	80	cm
	23 ½	26 ½	28 ¾	31 ½	in
Length to	32	37	42	45	cm
shoulder	12 ½	14 ½	16 ½	17 ¾	in
Sleeve	24	26	29	33	cm
length	9 ½	10 ¼	11 ½	13	in

MATERIALS

• 7(8:9:10) 50g/1 ¾oz balls of MillaMia Naturally Soft Merino in Storm (102) (M).
• 4(4:5:5) balls in contrast Seaside (161) (C).
• Pair each of 4.50mm (US 7) and 5 mm (US 8) knitting needles.

TENSION / GAUGE

18 sts and 24 rows to 10cm/4in square over st st using 5mm (US 8) needles and yarn double.

HINTS AND TIPS

A wonderful warm and comfortable striped hooded jumper. Knitted using the yarn double means that it is thick and cosy. Choosing a neutral main colour means that it will match well with most other clothes, a handy feature for an outerwear garment.

ABBREVIATIONS

See page 9.

NOTE

Use yarn double **throughout.**

SUGGESTED ALTERNATIVE COLOURWAYS

Scarlet	Midnight	Fawn	Peacock	Moss	Plum
140	101	160	144	103	162

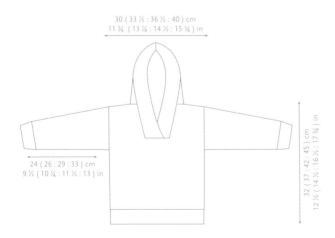

30 (33 ½ : 36 ½ : 40) cm
11 ¾ (13 ¼ : 14 ½ : 15 ¼) in

24 (26 : 29 : 33) cm
9 ½ (10 ¼ : 11 ½ : 13) in

32 (37 : 42 : 45) cm
12 ½ (14 ½ : 16 ½ : 17 ¾) in

BACK

With 4.50mm (US 7) needles and using C double cast on 56(62:68:74) sts.
1st row P2, [k4, p2] to end.
2nd row K2, [p4, k2] to end.
These 2 rows form the rib.
Work a further 6 rows.
Change to 5mm (US 8) needles.
Beg with a k row cont in st st and stripes of 4 rows C, and 6 rows M until back measures 32(37:42:45)cm/12 ½(14 ½:16 ½: 17 ¾)in from cast on edge, ending with a wrong side row.
Shape shoulders
Cast off 7(8:9:10) sts at beg of next 4 rows.
Cast off rem 28(30:32:34) sts.

FRONT

Work as given for back until front measures 20(23:26:28)cm/ 7 ¾(9:10 ¼:11)in from cast on edge, ending with a wrong side row.
Shape neck
Next row Patt 21(24:27:30) sts, turn and work on these sts for first side of neck.
Cont straight until front measures the same as back to shoulder shaping, ending at side edge.
Shape shoulder
Cast off 7(8:9:10) sts at beg of next and foll alt row.
Work 1 row.
Leave rem 7(8:9:10) sts on a holder.
With right side facing, cast off centre 14 sts, patt to end.
Cont straight until front measures the same as back to shoulder shaping, ending at side edge.
Shape shoulder
Cast off 7(8:9:10) sts at beg of next and foll alt row. 7(8:9:10) sts.
Leave these sts on a holder.

HOOD

Join shoulder seams.
With right side facing, using 5mm (US 8) needles and using M double, k across 7(8:9:10) sts on right front neck, cast on 50(52:58:60) sts, k across 7(8:9:10) sts on left front neck holder. 64(68:76:80) sts.
Next row P3, * k2, p2; rep from * to last 5 sts, k2, p3.
Next row K3, * p2, k2; rep from * to last 5 sts, p2, k3.
Rep the last 2 rows until hood measures 19(20:21:22)cm/ 7 ½(8:8 ¼:8 ¾)in, ending with a wrong side row.
Shape top
Next row Patt 32(34:38:40) sts, turn and work on these sts.
Cast off 4 sts at beg of next and 5(5:6:6) foll alt rows.
Work 1 row.
Cast off rem 8(10:10:12) sts.
Rejoin yarn to rem sts, complete to match first side.

SLEEVES

With 4.50mm (US 7) needles and using C double cast on 38(38:44:44) sts.
1st row P2, [k4, p2] to end.
2nd row K2, [p4, k2] to end.
These 2 rows form the rib.
Work a further 6 rows.
Change to 5mm (US 8) needles.
Beg with a k row cont in st st and stripes of 4 rows C, and 6 rows M.
Work 2 rows.
Inc row K3, m1, k to last 3 sts, m1, k3.
Work 5 rows.
Rep the last 6 rows 6(7:8:9) times more, and then the inc row again. 54(56:64:66) sts.
Cont straight until sleeve measures 24(26:29:33)cm/9 ½(10 ¼: 11 ½:13)in from cast on edge, ending with a wrong side row.
Cast off.

RIGHT FRONT BORDER

With right side facing using 4.50mm (US 7) needles and using M double, cast on one st, pick up and k74(82:90:98) sts along right front edge and right side of hood. 75(83:91:99) sts.
1st row [P2, k2] to last 3 sts, p3.
2nd row K3, [p2, k2] to end.
Rep the last 2 rows for 7 ½cm/3in ending with a 1st row.
Cast off in rib.

LEFT FRONT BORDER

With right side facing, using 4.50mm (US 7) needles and using M double, pick up and k74(82:90:98) sts along left side of hood and left front edge, cast on one st.
75(83:91:99) sts.
1st row P3, [k2, p2] to end.
2nd row [K2, p2] to last 3 sts, k3.
Rep the last 2 rows for 7 ½cm/3in ending with a 1st row.
Cast off in rib.

MAKE UP

With right sides together, fold hood in half and join shaped edge and borders. Sew cast on edge of hood to cast off sts on back neck. Lap right front border over left and sew to cast off edge at centre front. Sew on sleeves. Join side and sleeve seams.

TEDDY
BLANKET
OLLE
JUMPER
EMIL
BABYGROW
AND SOCKS

From left to right: **Teddy Blanket** in Peacock (144), Scarlet (140), Daisy Yellow (142), Grass (141) and Fuchsia (143) pattern on page 50, **Olle Jumper** in Midnight (101), Putty Grey (121), Peacock (144), Scarlet (140), Daisy Yellow (142) and Grass (141) pattern on page 44, **Emil Babygrow and Socks** in Storm (102), Putty Grey (121), Peacock (144), Scarlet (140), Daisy Yellow (142) and Grass (141) pattern on page 38

EMIL BABYGROW & SOCKS

SKILL LEVEL **Experienced**

SIZES / MEASUREMENTS

To fit age

Babygrow	0-3	3-6	6-12	mths
Socks		3-6	6-12	mths

ACTUAL GARMENT MEASUREMENTS

Chest	53	57	63	cm
	20 ¾	22 ½	25	in
Length to	44	48	53	cm
shoulder	17 ¼	19	21	in
Sleeve	14	16	18	cm
length	5 ½	6 ¼	7	in
Inside leg	12	14	17	cm
length	4 ¾	5 ½	6 ¾	in

MATERIALS

Babygrow

- 3(3:4) 50g/1 ¾oz balls of MillaMia Naturally Soft Merino in each of Storm (102) (M) and Putty Grey (121) (C).
- Small amounts of Peacock (144) (P), Daisy Yellow (142) (D), Grass (141) (G) and Scarlet (140) (S), left over from Socks.
- Pair each of 2.75mm (US 2) and 3.25mm (US 3) knitting needles.
- 5 buttons approx 15mm/ ⅝in diameter.

Socks

- One ball in each of Peacock (144) (P), Daisy Yellow (142) (D), Grass (141) (G) and Scarlet (140) (S).
- Small amount of Storm (102) (M), left over from Babygrow.
- Pair of 3.25mm (US 3) knitting needles.

TENSION / GAUGE

25 sts and 34 rows to 10cm/4in square over st st using 3.25mm (US 3) needles.

HINTS AND TIPS

A practical and fun all in one babygrow that will keep baby warm and snuggly when out and about. Bright and fun with the contrast button band, knitting the matching socks is a great way to make the most out of the yarn the pattern needs. We recommend you buy the buttons after you have knitted the button band so you can see the stripes in action before you decide on the best colour for your buttons.

ABBREVIATIONS

See page 9.

SUGGESTED ALTERNATIVE COLOURWAY

Snow	Fawn	Seaside	Plum	Forget	Petal
124	160	161	162	me not	122
				120	

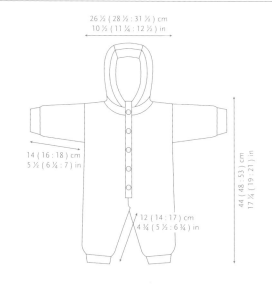

26 ½ (28 ½ : 31 ½) cm
10 ½ (11 ¼ : 12 ½) in

14 (16 : 18) cm
5 ½ (6 ¼ : 7) in

44 (48 : 53) cm
17 ¼ (19 : 21) in

12 (14 : 17) cm
4 ¾ (5 ½ : 6 ¾) in

LEFT LEG

With 2.75mm (US 2) needles and M, cast on 46(50:54) sts.
Rib row * K1, p1; rep from * to end.
Rep the last row for 2(3:4)cm/¾(1 ¼:1 ½)in, ending with a
right side row.
Inc row Rib 5(2:3) sts, * m1, rib 4(5:4); rep from * to last
5(3:3) sts, m1, rib 5(3:3). 56(60:67) sts.
Change to 3.25mm (US 3) needles.
Beg with a k row cont in st st, and stripes of 12 rows C and
12 rows M, **at the same time** inc one st at each end of the
3rd(3rd:5th) and every foll alt row until there are 86(92:99) sts.
Cont straight until leg measures 12(14:17)cm/4 ¾(5 ½:6 ¾)in,
ending with a p row. (Note patt row for working the right leg).
Shape crotch
Cast off 4 sts at beg of next 2 rows.
Dec one st at each end of next and 5 foll alt rows. 66(72:79) sts.
Work 1 row. **
Cut off yarn and leave sts on a holder.

RIGHT LEG

Work as given for left leg to **, ending at same patt row before
crotch.

MAIN PART

Work across sts of right leg then left leg. 132(144:158) sts.
Cont straight until work measures 5cm/2in from beg of crotch
shaping, ending with a p row.
Divide for opening
Cast off 3 sts at beg of next 2 rows. 126(138:152) sts.
Cont straight until work measures 32(35:38)cm/12 ½
(13 ¾:15)in from cast on edges, ending with a right side row.
Divide for armholes
Next row P31(34:38) turn and work on these sts for left front.

Left front
Cont on these sts for a further 9(10:12)cm/3 ½(4:4 ¾)in,
ending with a wrong side row.
Shape neck
K to last 7(8:9) sts, slip these sts on a holder.
Dec one st at neck edge on every row until 18(20:22) sts rem.
Cont straight until work measures 44(48:53)cm/17 ¼(19:21)in
from cast on edge, ending at armhole edge.
Shape shoulder
Cast off 9(10:11) sts at beg of next row.
Work 1 row.
Cast off rem 9(10:11) sts.
Back
With wrong side facing, join on yarn, p across next
64(70:76) sts, turn and work on these sts for back.
Cont straight until work measures 44(48:53)cm/17 ¼(19:21)in
from cast on edge, ending with a p row.
Shape shoulders
Cast off 9(10:11) sts at beg of next 4 rows.
Leave rem 28(30:32) sts on a holder.
Right front
With wrong side facing, join on yarn to next st, p to end.
31(34:38) sts.
Cont on these sts for a further 9(10:12)cm/3 ½(4:4 ¾)in,
ending with a wrong side row.
Break off yarn.
Shape neck
Slip 7(8:9) sts on a holder, join on yarn, then k to end.
Dec one st at neck edge on every row until 18(20:22) sts rem.
Cont straight until work measures 44(48:53)cm/17 ¼(19:21)in
from cast on edge, ending at armhole edge.
Shape shoulder
Cast off 9(10:11) sts at beg of next row.
Work 1 row.
Cast off rem 9(10:11) sts.

SLEEVES

With 2.75mm (US 2) needles and M, cast on 32(32:36) sts.
Rib row * K1, p1; rep from * to end.
Rep the last row for 3cm/1 ¼in, ending with a right side row.
Inc row Rib 4(2:2) sts, * m1, rib 3(2:2); rep from * to last 4(2:2) sts, m1, rib 4(2:2). 41(47:53) sts.
Change to 3.25mm (US 3) needles.
Beg with a k row cont in st st, and stripes of 6 rows C and 4 rows M, **at the same time** inc one st at each end of the 3rd and every foll alt row until there are 59(67:75) sts.
Cont straight until work measures 14(16:18)cm/5 ½(6 ¼:7)in from cast on edge, ending with a wrong side row.
Cast off.

HOOD

Join shoulder seams.
With right side facing, using 2.75mm (US 2) needles and M, k7(8:9) sts from holder, pick up and k16 sts up right side of front neck, inc one st at centre k across sts from back neck, pick up and k16 sts down left side of front neck, k7(8:9) sts from holder. 75(79:83) sts.
Next row P1, * k1, p1; rep from * to end.
Next row K1, * p1, k1; rep from * to end.
Rep the last 2 rows twice more.
Next row Rib 6(7:8) and slip these sts onto a safety pin, rib 7(8:9), * m1, rib 7; rep from * to last 13(15:17) sts, m1, rib 7(8:9), slip last 6(7:8) sts onto a safety pin. 71(73:75) sts.
Change to 3.25mm (US 3) needles.
Beg with a k row cont in st st, and stripes of 6 rows C and 4 rows M, until hood measures 12(14:16)cm/4 ¾(5 ½:6 ¼)in, ending with a p row.
Shape top
Next row K46(47:48), turn.
Next row Sl 1, p19, p2 tog, turn.
Next row Sl 1, k19, skpo, turn.

Rep the last 2 rows until all sts are worked off each side of centre sts.
Leave rem 21 sts on a holder.

HOOD EDGING

With wrong side facing, using 2.75mm (US 2) needles, rejoin M to inner edge of 6(7:8) sts from right side of hood, rib to end.
Next row Rib sts from right side of hood, pick up and k29(33:37) sts up right side of hood, k centre 21 sts, pick up and k 29(33:37) sts down left side of hood and rib 6(7:8) sts from left side of hood. 91(101:111) sts.
Rib 7 rows.
Cast off in rib.

BUTTONHOLE BAND

With right side facing, using 2.75 mm (US 2) needles, pick up and k14(16:18) sts in each of P, D, G, S, P up right side of front opening to neck. 70(80:90) sts.
Twisting yarns on wrong side to avoid a hole, work 3 rows in rib.
Buttonhole row Rib 6(7:8), [k2 tog, yf, rib (12:14:16) sts] 4 times, k2 tog, yf, rib 6(7:8).
Rib 3 rows.
Cast off in rib.

BUTTON BAND

With right side facing, using 2.75 mm (US 2) needles, pick up and k14(16:18) sts in each of P, S, G, D, P down left side of front opening. 70(80:90) sts.
Twisting yarns on wrong side to avoid a hole, work 7 rows rib.
Cast off in rib.

MAKE UP

Sew on sleeves. Join leg and crotch seams. Sew on buttons.

SOCKS

With 3.25mm (US 3) needles and M cast on 38(42) sts.
1st rib row K2, * p2, k2; rep from * to end.
2nd rib row P2, * k2, p2; rep from * to end.
Rep the last 2 rows twice more.
Beg with a k row, cont in st st and stripes of 4 rows P,
4 rows D, 4 rows G and 4 rows S.
Work 2(4) rows.
Dec row K5, k2 tog, k to last 7 sts, skpo, k5.
Work 3(5) rows.
Dec row K5, k2 tog, k to last 7 sts, skpo, k5.
Work 3(5) rows.
Dec row K4, k2 tog, k to last 6 sts, skpo, k4.
Work 3(5) rows.
Dec row K3, [k2 tog, k6(7)] 3 times, k2 tog, k3(4). 28(32) sts.
Work 1 row.
Cont in M only.
Shape heel
Next row K8(9) sts only, turn.
Work 9 rows in st st on these 8(9) sts.
Dec row K2(3), k2 tog tbl, k1, turn.
Next row Sl 1, p3(4).
Dec row K3(4), k2 tog tbl, k1, turn.
Next row Sl 1, p4(5).
Dec row K4(5), k2 tog tbl, turn.
Next row Sl 1, p4(5). Break off yarn, leave these sts on a holder.
With right side facing, slip next 12(14) sts on a holder, rejoin M
to rem sts, k to end.
Next row P8(9) sts only, turn.
Work 9 rows in st st on these 8(9) sts only.
Dec row P2(3), p2 tog, p1, turn.
Next row Sl 1, k3(4).
Dec row P3(4), p2 tog, p1, turn.
Next row Sl 1, k4(5).
Dec row P4(5), p2 tog, break yarn.
Leave rem 5(6) sts on a holder.
Cont in stripes, rejoin P(G).

Shape instep
Next row With right side facing, k5(6) sts from first holder,
pick up and k8 sts evenly along inside edge of heel, k12(14) sts
from holder, pick up and k8 sts along inside edge of heel and
k5(6) sts from holder. 38(42) sts.
P 1 row.
Dec row K11(12), k2 tog, k12(14), k2 tog tbl, k11(12).
P 1 row.
Dec row K10(11), k2 tog, k12(14), k2 tog tbl, k10(11).
P 1 row.
Dec row K9(10), k2 tog, k12(14), k2 tog tbl, k9(10).
P 1 row.
Dec row K8(9), k2 tog, k12(14), k2 tog tbl, k8(9). 30(34) sts.
Work 11(15) rows straight.
Shape toe
Cont in M only.
Dec row K1, [k2 tog tbl, k5(6)] 4 times, k1.
P 1 row.
Dec row K1, [k2 tog tbl, k4(5)] 4 times, k1.
P 1 row.
Dec row K1, [k2 tog tbl, k3(4)] 4 times, k1.
P 1 row.
Dec row K1, [k2 tog tbl, k2(3)] 4 times, k1.
2nd size only
P 1 row.
Dec row K1, [k2 tog tbl, k2] 4 times, k1.
Both sizes
Dec row [P2 tog tbl] 7 times.
Break off yarn, thread through rem sts, pull up and secure. Join
seam.

OLLE JUMPER & HAT

SKILL LEVEL **Beginner / Improving**

SIZES / MEASUREMENTS

To fit age

Jumper	3-6	6-9	9-12	12-18	18-24	mths
Hat	3-9		9-18		18-24	mths

ACTUAL GARMENT MEASUREMENTS

Chest	51	54	57	61	64	cm
	20	21	22 ½	24	25	in
Length to	24	26	28	32	36	cm
shoulder	9 ½	10 ¼	11	12 ½	14 ¼	in
Sleeve	15	17	19	22	24	cm
length	6	6 ¾	7 ½	8 ½	9 ½	in

MATERIALS

Jumper

- 2(2:2:3:3) 50g/1 ¾oz balls of MillaMia Naturally Soft Merino in Putty Grey (121) (M).
- 1(1:1:2:2) balls in contrast Midnight (101) (C).
- Small amounts of Peacock (144) (P), Daisy Yellow (142) (D), Grass (141) (G) and Scarlet (140) (S), left over from Hat.
- Pair each of 3mm (US 2) and 3.25mm (US 3) knitting needles.
- 4 buttons approx 15mm/⅝in diameter.

Hat

- One ball in each of Peacock (144) (P), Daisy Yellow (142) (D), Grass (141) (G) and Scarlet (140) (S).
- Small amount of Midnight (101) (C), left over from Jumper.
- Pair of 3.25mm (US 3) knitting needles.

TENSION / GAUGE

25 sts and 34 rows to 10cm/4in square over st st using 3.25mm (US 3) needles.

HINTS AND TIPS

Put your own stamp on this jumper by selecting your own preferred colourway for the button band. The raglan sleeve offers a lovely decorative element and makes a feature of the stripes on the body and sleeves. Make the most out of your yarn purchase by knitting the matching hat and see also the Emil Socks.

ABBREVIATIONS

See page 9.

SUGGESTED ALTERNATIVE COLOURWAY

Snow	Fawn	Seaside	Plum	Forget	Petal
124	160	161	162	me not	122
				120	

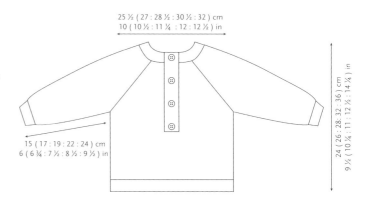

25 ½ (27 : 28 ½ : 30 ½ : 32) cm
10 (10 ½ : 11 ¼ : 12 : 12 ½) in

15 (17 : 19 : 22 : 24) cm
6 (6 ¾ : 7 ½ : 8 ½ : 9 ½) in

24 (26 : 28 : 32 : 36) cm
9 ½ (10 ¼ : 11 : 12 ½ : 14 ¼) in

BACK

With 3mm (US 2) needles and C, cast on 66(70:74:78:82) sts.
1st rib row K2, [p2, k2] to end.
2nd rib row P2, [k2, p2] to end.
Rep the last 2 rows twice more.
Join on M.
Change to 3.25mm (US 3) needles.
Beg with a k row, cont in st st and stripes of 12 rows M and 12 rows C until back measures approx 14(15:16:19:22)cm/ 5 ½(6:6 ¼:7 ½:8 ¾)in from cast on edge, ending with 6(10:2:12:10) rows C(C:M:M:C).
Shape armholes
Cast off 4 sts at beg of next 2 rows. 58(62:66:70:74) sts.
Next row K2, skpo, k to last 4 sts, k2 tog, k2.
Next row P to end.
Rep the last 2 rows until 26(28:30:32:34) sts rem.
Cast off.

FRONT

Work as given for back until 8(6:12:10:16) rows less than back to armhole shaping have been worked.
Divide for front opening
Next row K30(32:33:35:36) turn and work on these sts for first side of neck shaping.
Cont in patt until front measures same as back to armhole shaping, ending with a wrong side row.
Shape armhole
Cast off 4 sts at beg of next row. 26(28:29:31:32) sts.
Next row P to end.
Next row K2, skpo, k to end.
Next row P to end.
Rep the last 2 rows until 10(11:11:12:12) sts rem.
Cast off.
With right side facing, rejoin yarn to rem sts, cast off 6(6:8:8:10) sts, k to end.

Cont in patt until front measures same as back to armhole shaping, ending with a right side row.
Shape armhole
Cast off 4 sts at beg of next row. 26(28:29:31:32) sts.
Next row K to last 4 sts, k2 tog, k2.
Next row P to end.
Rep the last 2 rows until 10(11:11:12:12) sts rem.
Cast off.

SLEEVES

With 3mm (US 2) needles and C cast on 34(34:38:42:46) sts.
1st rib row K2, [p2, k2] to end.
2nd rib row P2, [k2, p2] to end.
Work 2 rows M, 2 rows C.
Change to 3.25mm (US 3) needles.
Beg with a k row, cont in st st beg 4(4:0:0:4) rows C and then stripes of 8 rows M and 4 rows C.
Work 2 rows.
Inc row K3, m1, k to last 3 sts, m1, k3.
Work 5 rows.
Rep the last 6 rows 4(6:7:8:9) times more and then the inc row again. 46(50:56:62:68) sts.
Cont straight until sleeve measures approx 15(17:19:22:24)cm/ 6(6 ¾:7 ½:8 ½:9 ½)in from cast on edge, ending with 6(2:2:4:2) rows M(C:M:C:C).
Shape sleeve top
Cast off 4 sts at beg of next 2 rows. 38(42:48:54:60) sts.
Next row K2, skpo, k to last 4 sts, k2 tog, k2.
Next row P to end.
Next row K to end.
Next row P to end.
Rep the last 4 rows 4(4:3:2:1) times more.
Next row K2, skpo, k to last 4 sts, k2 tog, k2.
Next row P to end.
Rep the last 2 rows until 16(18:20:22:24) sts rem.
Cast off.

NECKBAND

Join raglan seams.

With right side facing, using 3mm (US 2) needles and C, pick up and k9(10:10:11:11) sts from right front neck edge, 13(15:18:20:23) sts from right sleeve, 24(26:28:30:32) sts from back neck, 13(15:18:20:23) sts from left sleeve, 9(10:10:11:11) sts from left front neck edge. 68(76:84:92:100) sts.

1st row P3, [k2, p2] to last 5 sts, k2, p3.

2nd row K3, [p2, k2] to last 5 sts, p2, k3.

Rep the last 2 rows twice more and the 1st row again.

Cast off in rib.

BUTTONHOLE BAND

With right side facing, using 3mm (US 2) needles, pick up and k5(5:6:6:7) sts in each of P, D, G, S, P, D, G evenly up right front opening and neckband edge. 35(35:42:42:49) sts.

Twisting yarns on wrong side to avoid a hole, beg with a p row, work 4(4:5:5:6) rows st st.

1st, 2nd and 5th sizes only

Buttonhole row P2(2:3), yrn, p2 tog, [p8(8:12), yrn, p2 tog] 3 times, p1(1:2).

3rd and 4th sizes only

Buttonhole row K3, yf, k2 tog, [k10, yf, k2 tog] 3 times, k1.

All sizes

Work 4(4:5:5:6) rows.

Cast off.

BUTTON BAND

With right side facing, using 3mm (US 2) needles pick up and k5(5:6:6:7) sts in each of G,D,P,S,G,D,P evenly down neckband edge and left front opening. 35(35:42:42:49) sts.

Twisting yarns on wrong side to avoid a hole, beg with a p row, work 9(9:11:11:13) rows st st.

Cast off.

TO MAKE UP

Join side and sleeve seams. Lap buttonhole band over button band and sew to cast off edge at centre front. Sew on buttons.

HAT

With 3.25mm (US 3) needles and C, cast on 92(101:110) sts.
Starting with a k row work 14 rows st st.
Beg with a k row, cont in st st and stripes of 4 rows P, 4 rows
D, 4 rows G and 4 rows S until hat measures 14(15:16)cm/
5 ½(6:6 ¼)in from cast on edge, ending with a p row.

Shape crown
1st row [K8(9:10), k2 tog] 9 times, k2.
2nd row P to end.
3rd row [K7(8:9), k2 tog] 9 times, k2.
4th row P to end.
5th row [K6(7:8), k2 tog] 9 times, k2.
6th row P to end.
7th row [K5(6:7), k2 tog] 9 times, k2.
8th row P to end.
9th row [K4(5:6), k2 tog] 9 times, k2.
10th row P to end.
11th row [K3(4:5), k2 tog] 9 times, k2.
12th row P to end.
13th row [K2(3:4), k2 tog] 9 times, k2.
14th row P to end.
15th row [K1(2:3), k2 tog] 9 times, k2.
16th row P to end.

2nd and 3rd sizes only
17th row [K(1:2), k2 tog] 9 times, k2.
18th row P to end.

3rd size only
19th row [K(1), k2 tog] 9 times, k2.
20th row P to end.

All sizes
Next row [K2 tog] 10 times.
Next row [P2 tog] 5 times.
Leaving a long end, cut off yarn and thread through rem sts,
pull up and secure.
Join seam, reversing seam on first 14 rows for roll up brim.

TEDDY BLANKET

SKILL LEVEL Beginner

SIZES / MEASUREMENTS

To fit   One size for pram or cot

ACTUAL MEASUREMENTS

Length   92 ½   cm
                36 ½   in

Width   75   cm
                29 ½   in

MATERIALS

- Three 50g/1 ¾oz balls of MillaMia Naturally Soft Merino in each of colours Daisy Yellow (142) (D) and Grass (141) (G).
- Two balls in each of Fuchsia (143) (F) and Scarlet (140) (S).
- Four balls of Peacock (144) (P).
- Circular 3.25mm (US 3) knitting needle – ideally 80cm/29in or 100cm/40in long.

TENSION / GAUGE

25 sts and 50 rows to 10cm/4in over garter st using 3.25mm (US 3) needles.

HINTS AND TIPS

A bright fun blanket. An ideal gift for a newborn with its use of optimistic colours in playful stripes. Big enough to use in the pram, buggy or cot. Garter stitch is so quick and easy making this a relaxing and rewarding knit. Using long circular needles makes it easier to manage the width of the blanket.

ABBREVIATIONS

See page 9.

SUGGESTED ALTERNATIVE COLOURWAY

Midnight   Snow   Seaside   Plum   Forget
101   124   161   162   me not
                                    120

NOTE

Slip the first stitch of **each** row to create a firmer edge.

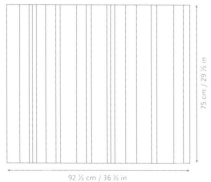

75 cm / 29 ½ in

92 ½ cm / 36 ½ in

BLANKET

With 3.25mm (US 3) circular needle and P, cast on 187 sts.

1st row Sl1, k to end.

2nd row Sl1, k to end.

These rows set the g-st patt.

Cont in g-st for a further 38 rows.

Switch to F and cont in g-st for 26 rows.

Switch to D and cont in g-st for 10 rows.

Switch to G and cont in g-st for 10 rows.

Switch to S and cont in g-st for 26 rows.

Switch to P and cont in g-st for 26 rows.

Switch to F and cont in g-st for 10 rows.

Switch to D and cont in g-st for 40 rows.

Switch to G and cont in g-st for 26 rows.

Switch to S and cont in g-st for 10 rows.

Switch to P and cont in g-st for 40 rows.

Switch to F and cont in g-st for 10 rows.

Switch to D and cont in g-st for 10 rows.

Switch to G and cont in g-st for 26 rows.

Switch to S and cont in g-st for 26 rows.

Switch to P and cont in g-st for 40 rows.

Switch to F and cont in g-st for 10 rows.

Switch to D and cont in g-st for 40 rows.

Switch to G and cont in g-st for 26 rows.

Switch to S and cont in g-st for 10 rows.

Cast off using S and sew in ends.

CARLOTA
DRESS
FELICIA
CARDIGAN
FABIAN
TOP

From left to right: **Carlota Dress**
in Midnight (101), Petal (122), Scarlet (140),
Lilac Blossom (123), Daisy Yellow (142), Grass
(141), Fuchsia (143), Seaside (161), Claret
(104) and Plum (162) pattern on page 66,
Felicia Cardigan in Midnight (101), Scarlet
(140), Lilac Blossom (123), Seaside (161) and
Daisy Yellow (142) pattern on page 56,
Fabian Top in Midnight (101), Scarlet (140),
Forget me not (120) and Seaside (161)
pattern on page 62

FELICIA CARDIGAN

SKILL LEVEL **Experienced**

SIZES / MEASUREMENTS

To fit age	6-12	12-24	24-36	36-48	48-60	mths

ACTUAL GARMENT MEASUREMENTS

Chest	57	60	63	66	69	cm
	22 ½	23 ½	24 ¾	26	27	in
Length to	28	31	34	38	42	cm
shoulder	11	12 ¼	13 ¼	15	16 ½	in
Sleeve	17	19	22	24	28	cm
length	6 ¾	7 ½	8 ¾	9 ½	11	in

MATERIALS

- 2(3:3:3:4) 50g/1 ¾oz balls of MillaMia Naturally Soft Merino in main colour Lilac Blossom (123) (M).
- Two balls of Seaside (161) (C).
- One ball in each of Scarlet (140) (A), Midnight (101) and Daisy Yellow (142).
- Pair each of 3mm (US 2) and 3.25mm (US 3) knitting needles.
- Circular 3mm (US 2) knitting needle.
- Two buttons approx 21mm/⅞ in diameter.

TENSION / GAUGE

25 sts and 34 rows to 10cm/4in square over st st using 3.25mm (US 3) needles.

HINTS AND TIPS

Stick to bright, strongly contrasting colours to maximise the effect of this deliberately mismatched cardigan design. It attains the high impact of a colourwork item through the presence of the fun patterns on the left front and right sleeve. At the same time limiting the amount of colourwork to a few areas makes it a great introduction for those that do not have the desire to knit a whole item using this technique.

ABBREVIATIONS

See page 9.

SUGGESTED ALTERNATIVE COLOURWAY

Plum	Forget	Grass	Claret	Daisy
162	me not	141	104	Yellow
	120			142

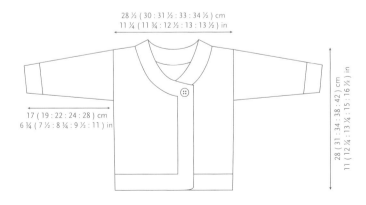

28 ½ (30 : 31 ½ : 33 : 34 ½) cm
11 ¼ (11 ¾ : 12 ½ : 13 : 13 ½) in

17 (19 : 22 : 24 : 28) cm
6 ¾ (7 ½ : 8 ¾ : 9 ½ : 11) in

28 (31 : 34 : 38 : 42) cm
11 (12 ¼ : 13 ¼ : 15 : 16 ½) in

BACK

With 3mm (US 2) needles and C cast on 73(77:81:85:89) sts.

Moss st row K1, [p1, k1] to end.

Rep the last row 17 times more.

Break off C.

Join on M.

Change to 3.25mm (US 3) needles.

Beg with a k row, work in st st until back measures
23(26:29:33:37)cm/9(10 ¼:11 ¼:13:14 ½)in from cast on edge,
ending with a p row.

Shape back neck

Next row K29(30:31:32:33), turn and work on these sts for first
side of neck shaping.

Dec one st at neck edge of next 10 rows. 19(20:21:22:23) sts.

Work 5 rows.

Shape shoulder

Cast off 9(10:10:11:11) sts at beg of next row.

Work 1 row.

Cast off rem 10(10:11:11:12) sts.

With right side facing slip centre 15(17:19:21:23) sts onto a
holder, rejoin yarn to rem sts, k to end.

Dec one st at neck edge of next 10 rows. 19(20:21:22:23) sts.

Work 6 rows.

Shape shoulder

Cast off 9(10:10:11:11) sts at beg of next row.

Work 1 row.

Cast off rem 10(10:11:11:12) sts.

CHART A

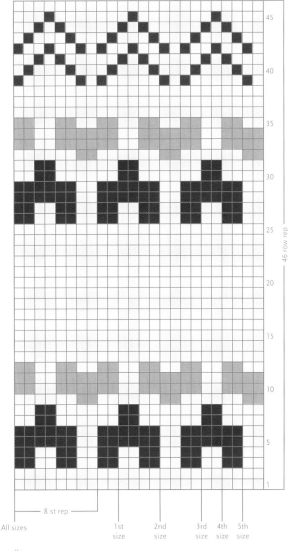

Key

Lilac Blossom (123)
Scarlet (140)
Seaside (161)
Midnight (101)
Daisy Yellow (142)

LEFT FRONT

With 3mm (US 2) needles and C cast on 55(59:63:65:67) sts.

Moss st row K1, [p1, k1] to end.

Rep the last row 17 times more.

Change to 3.25mm (US 3) needles.

Break off C.

Work in patt from Chart A with moss st border as follows.

Next row (right side) Patt to last 13 sts, join on C, moss st 13C.

Next row Moss st 13C, patt to end.

These 2 rows form the patt with moss st border.

Work straight rep 46 chart rows until front measures 16(18:20:23:26)cm/6 ¼ (7:8:9:10 ¼)in from cast on edge, ending with a wrong side row.

Shape neck

Next row Patt to last 13 sts, leave these sts on a holder.

Next row Cast off 5 sts, patt to end.

Next row Patt to end.

Next row Cast off 4 sts, patt to end.

Next row Patt to end.

Next row Cast off 3 sts, patt to end.

Next row Patt to end.

Next row Cast off 2 sts, patt to end.

Next row Patt to end.

Next row P2 tog, patt to end.

Rep the last 2 rows until 19(20:21:22:23) sts rem.

Cont straight until front measures same as back to shoulder, ending at armhole edge.

Shape shoulder

Cast off 9(10:10:11:11) sts at beg of next row.

Work 1 row.

Cast off rem 10(10:11:11:12) sts.

RIGHT FRONT

With 3mm (US 2) needles and C cast on 55(59:63:65:67) sts.

Moss st row K1, [p1, k1] to end.

Rep the last row 17 times more.

Change to 3.25mm (US 3) needles.

1st row (right side) Moss st 13C, join on M, k to end.

2nd row With M, p to last 13 sts, moss st 13C.

3rd to 6th rows Rep 1st and 2nd rows twice more.

7th row Moss st 13C, join on A, k to end.

8th row With A, p to last 13 sts, moss st 13C.

9th and 10th rows As 7th and 8th rows.

These 10 rows form the stripe patt with moss st border.

Work straight until front measures 16(18:20:23:26)cm/6 ¼ (7:8:9:10 ¼)in from cast on edge, ending with a wrong side row.

Shape neck

Next row With C, moss st 13, leave these 13 sts on a holder, then patt to end.

Next row Patt to end.

Next row Cast off 5 sts, patt to end.

Next row Patt to end.

Next row Cast off 4 sts, patt to end.

Next row Patt to end.

Next row Cast off 3 sts, patt to end.

Next row Patt to end.

Next row Cast off 2 sts, patt to end.

Next row Patt to end.

Next row Skpo, patt to end.

Rep the last 2 rows until 19(20:21:22:23) sts rem.

Cont straight until front measures same as back to shoulder, ending at armhole edge.

Shape shoulder

Cast off 9(10:10:11:11) sts at beg of next row.

Work 1 row.

Cast off rem 10(10:11:11:12) sts.

LEFT SLEEVE

With 3mm (US 2) needles and C cast on 25(27:31:35:37) sts.
Moss st row K1, [p1, k1] to end.
Rep the last row 17 times more, inc one st at centre of last row.
26(28:32:36:38) sts.
Change to 3.25mm (US 3) needles.
Beg with a k row, cont in st st and stripes of 6 rows M and 4 rows A.
Work 2 rows.
Inc row K3, m1, k to last 3 sts, m1, k3.
Work 3 rows.
Inc row K3, m1, k to last 3 sts, m1, k3.
Work 1(1:1:1:3) rows.
Rep the last 6(6:6:6:8) rows 5(6:6:8:8) times more and then the
inc row 0(0:1:0:1) times again. 50(56:62:72:76) sts.
Cont straight until sleeve measures 17(19:22:24:28)cm/6 ¾
(7 ½: 8 ¾:9 ½:11)in from cast on edge, ending with a p row.
Cast off.

RIGHT SLEEVE

Work as given for left sleeve but after moss st border, work in
patt from Chart B instead of stripes.

NECKBAND

Join shoulder seams.
With right side facing, using 3mm (US 2) circular needle, slip
13 sts from right front holder onto a needle, using C pick up
and k14 sts from cast off sts up right front, 24(27:30:33:36)
sts up right front neck, 13 sts down right back neck,
k15(17:19:21:23) sts from back neck, pick up and k13 sts up
left side of back neck, 24(27:30:33:36) sts down left front neck,
14 sts from left front cast off sts, moss st across 13 sts on left
front holder.
Moss st 7 rows.
1st buttonhole row [K1, p1] 3 times, k2 tog, y2rn, skpo,
moss st to last 10 sts, k2 tog, y2rn, skpo, [p1, k1] 3 times.

CHART B

14 st rep

10 row rep

2nd size   3rd size   4th size   5th size   1st size

Key
■ Midnight (101)
□ Lilac Blossom (123)

2nd buttonhole row Moss st to end, working twice into y2rn,
working second loop tbl.
Moss st 7 rows.
Cast off in moss st.

MAKE UP

Sew on sleeves. Join side and sleeve seams. Sew on buttons.

FABIAN TOP

SKILL LEVEL **Improving**

SIZES / MEASUREMENTS

To fit age	1-2	2-3	3-4	4-5	years

ACTUAL GARMENT MEASUREMENTS

Chest	58	64	70	77	cm
	23	25	27 ½	30 ½	in
Length to	34	39	44	49	cm
shoulder	13 ¼	15 ¼	17 ¼	19 ¼	in
Sleeve	19	21	24	28	cm
length	7 ½	8 ¼	9 ½	11	in

MATERIALS

- 2(2:3:3) 50g/1 ¾oz balls of MillaMia Naturally Soft Merino in each of Forget me not (120) (A) and Seaside (161) (B).
- One ball of Midnight (101) (C).
- One ball of Scarlet (140) (D).
- Pair each of 3mm (US 2) and 3.25mm (US 3) knitting needles.

TENSION / GAUGE

25 sts and 34 rows to 10cm/4in square over st st using 3.25mm (US 3) needles.

HINTS AND TIPS

Simple yet stylish, this jumper suits playful little boys of all ages. To help you cast off loosely for the neckband you can try using a larger size needle in your right hand when casting off.

ABBREVIATIONS

See page 9.

NOTE

Work in Stripe Sequence **throughout**.

STRIPE SEQUENCE

6 rows Forget me not (120) (A) and 6 rows Seaside (161) (B).

SUGGESTED ALTERNATIVE COLOURWAYS

Snow	Midnight	Grass	Scarlet		Putty	Storm	Daisy	Peacock
124	101	141	140		Grey	102	Yellow	144
					121		142	

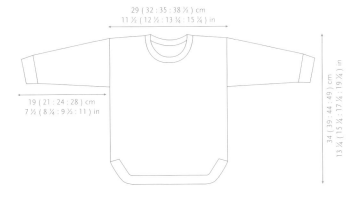

29 (32 : 35 : 38 ½) cm
11 ½ (12 ½ : 13 ¾ : 15 ¼) in

19 (21 : 24 : 28) cm
7 ½ (8 ¼ : 9 ½ : 11) in

34 (39 : 44 : 49) cm
13 ¼ (15 ¼ : 17 ¼ : 19 ¼) in

BACK

With 3.25mm (US 3) needles and A cast on 50(58:66:74) sts.
Beg with a k row cont in st st and stripe sequence.
Work 2 rows.
Inc row K1, m1, k to last st, m1, k1.
Next row P to end.
Rep the last 2 rows 6 times more. 64(72:80:88) sts.
Cast on 5 sts at beg of next 2 rows. 74(82:90:98) sts.
Beg with a k row cont in st st until back measures 21(25:29:33)cm/
8 ¼(10:11 ½:13)in from cast on edge, ending with a p row.
Shape armholes
Cast off 6(7:8:9) sts at beg of next 2 rows. 62(68:74:80) sts.
Work straight until back measures 30(35:40:45)cm/11 ¾
(13 ¾:15 ¾:17 ¾)in from cast on edge, ending with a p row.
Shape back neck
Next row K20(22:24:26), turn and work on these sts.
Dec one st at neck edge on next 4 rows. 16(18:20:22) sts.
Work 1 row.
Shape shoulder
Cast off 8(9:10:11) sts at the beg of next row.
Work 1 row.
Cast off rem 8(9:10:11) sts.
With right side facing slip centre 22(24:26:28) sts on a holder,
rejoin yarn to rem sts, k to end.
Dec one st at neck edge on next 4 rows. 16(18:20:22) sts.
Work 2 rows.
Shape shoulder
Cast off 8(9:10:11) sts at the beg of next row.
Work 1 row.
Cast off rem 8(9:10:11) sts.

FRONT

Work as given for back until front measures 27(32:37:42)cm/
10 ½(12 ½:14 ½:16 ½)in from cast on edge, ending with
a p row.
Shape front neck
Next row K23(25:27:29), turn and work on these sts.
Dec one st at neck edge on next 7 rows. 16(18:20:22) sts.
Work straight until front measures same as back to shoulder
shaping, ending at armhole edge.
Shape shoulder
Cast off 8(9:10:11) sts at the beg of next row.
Work 1 row.
Cast off rem 8(9:10:11) sts.
With right side facing slip centre 16(18:20:22) sts on a holder,
rejoin yarn to rem sts, k to end.
Dec one st at neck edge on next 7 rows. 16(18:20:22) sts.
Work straight until front measures same as back to shoulder
shaping, ending at armhole edge.
Shape shoulder
Cast off 8(9:10:11) sts at the beg of next row.
Work 1 row.
Cast off rem 8(9:10:11) sts.

SLEEVES

With 3mm (US 2) needles and D cast on 42(50:58:66) sts.
1st row K3, [p4, k4] to last 7 sts, p4, k3.
2nd row P3, [k4, p4] to last 7 sts, k4, p3.
Rep the last 2 rows 5(6:7:8) times more.
Change to 3.25mm (US 3) needles.
Beg with a k row, 6 rows B and then cont stripe sequence.
Work 2(4:6:10) rows st st.
Inc row K3, m1, k to last 3 sts, m1, k3.
Work 7(9:13:17) rows.
Rep the last 8(10:14:18) rows 5(4:3:2) times more and then the inc row again. 56(62:68:74) sts.
Cont straight until sleeve measures approx 19(21:24:28)cm/ 7 ½(8 ¼:9 ½:11)in from cast on edge, ending with 6(4:2:6) rows B(A:A:B).
Mark each end of last row with a coloured thread.
Work a further 6(8:10:12) rows.
Cast off.

NECKBAND

Join right shoulder seam.
With right side facing, 3mm (US 2) needles and C, pick up and k20(22:24:26) sts down left side of front neck, k16(18:20:22) sts on front neck holder, pick up and k20(22:24:26) sts up right side of front neck, 10 sts down right side of back neck, k22(24:26:28) sts on back neck holder, pick up and k10 sts up left side of back neck. 98(106:114:122) sts.
1st row K3, [p4, k4] to last 7 sts, p4, k3.
2nd row P3, [k4, p4] to last 7 sts, k4, p3.
Rep the last 2 rows 3(3:4:4) times more and the 1st row again.
Cast off loosely in rib.

LOWER BORDER (back and front alike)

With right side facing, 3mm (US 2) needles and C beg at top of shaped edge (after cast on sts), pick up and k12 sts down slope, 50(58:66:74) sts along bottom and 12 sts up slope on other side.
1st row K3, p4, k4, p8, [k4, p4] to last 23 sts, k4, p8, k4, p4, k3. This row sets the rib.
2nd row Rib 14 as set, inc in each of next 2 sts, rib to last 16 sts, inc in each of next 2 sts, rib to end.
3rd row Rib 15, k2, patt to last 17 sts, k2, rib to end.
4th row Rib15, inc in each of next 2 sts, rib to last 17 sts, inc in each of next 2 sts, rib to end.
5th row Rib to end.
6th row Rib 15, inc in next st, p2, inc in next st, rib to last 19 sts, inc in next, p2, inc in next st, rib to end.
7th row Rib 15, k6, rib to last 21 sts, k6, rib to end.
Cast off in rib as set.

TO MAKE UP

Join left shoulder and neckband seam. Sew in sleeves placing rows above coloured threads to cast off sts underarm.
Join side and sleeve seams. Sew row ends of lower border to cast on sts on body.

CARLOTA DRESS

SKILL LEVEL **Beginner / Improving**

SIZES / MEASUREMENTS

To fit age	1-2	2-3	3-4	4-5	years

ACTUAL GARMENT MEASUREMENTS

Chest	58	62	67	72	cm
	23	24 ½	26 ½	28 ½	in
Length to	45	50	56	64	cm
shoulder	17 ¾	19 ¾	22	25	in
Sleeve	5	6	7	7 ½	cm
length	2	2 ¼	2 ¾	3	in

MATERIALS

- 1(1:2:2) 50g/1 ¾oz balls of MillaMia Naturally Soft Merino in Midnight (101).
- One ball in each of Petal (122), Scarlet (140), Lilac Blossom (123), Daisy Yellow (142), Grass (141), Fuchsia (143), Seaside (161), Claret (104), Plum (162).
- Pair each of 3mm (US 2) and 3.25mm (US 3) knitting needles.

TENSION / GAUGE

25 sts and 34 rows to 10cm/4in square over st st using 3.25mm (US 3) needles.

HINTS AND TIPS

A riot of colour, this dress is comfortable and loose fitting with clashing striped pockets as an added feature. Make a separate note of the stripe sequence required for the size you are knitting to get organised before you start.

STRIPE SEQUENCE

4(4:6:8) rows Petal, 13(15:17:19) rows Scarlet, 14(16:18:20) rows Lilac Blossom, 8(9:10:12) rows Daisy Yellow, 4(4:5:6) rows Midnight, 6(7:8:10) rows Grass, 9(10:12:14) rows Fuchsia, 12(14:16:18) rows Seaside, 6(6:7:9) rows Claret, 10(12:14:16) rows Plum, 4(5:6:7) rows Petal, 12(14:16:18) rows Scarlet, 4(4:5:7) rows Lilac Blossom, 6(7:8:9) rows Daisy Yellow, 7(8:9:10) rows Midnight, 7(8:9:10) rows Grass, 6(7:8:9) rows Fuchsia, 4(4:5:5) rows Seaside, then cont in Claret.

ABBREVIATIONS

See page 9.

SUGGESTED ALTERNATIVE COLOURWAY

| Moss 103 | Petal 122 | Peacock 144 | Fawn 160 | Seaside 161 | Storm 102 | Claret 104 | Snow 124 | Fuchsia 143 | Forget me not 120 |

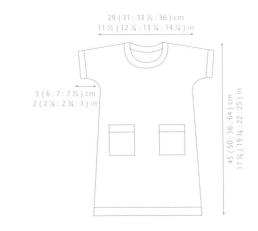

29 (31 : 33 ½ : 36) cm
11 ½ (12 ¼ : 13 ¼ : 14 ¼) in

5 (6 : 7 : 7 ½) cm
2 (2 ¼ : 2 ¾ : 3) in

45 (50 : 56 : 64) cm
17 ¾ (19 ¾ : 22 : 25) in

BACK

With 3.25mm (US 3) needles and Midnight cast on 98(110:122:134) sts.
1st row K2, [p4, k2] to end.
2nd row P2, [k4, p2] to end.
Rep the last 2 rows 5 times.
Beg with a k row cont in st st and stripe sequence.
Work 2 rows.
Dec row K4, skpo, k to last 6 sts, k2 tog, k4.
Work 7 rows.
Rep the last 8 rows 10(13:16:19) times more and then the dec row again. 74(80:86:92) sts.
Work straight until back measures approx 34(38:44:51)cm/ 13 ½(15:17 ½:20)in from cast on edge, ending with 4(4:5:7) rows Lilac Blossom.
Shape sleeves
Cont in stripes.
Cast on 2 sts at beg of next 2 rows and 3(4:5:6) sts at beg of foll 4 rows. 90(100:110:120) sts.
Work straight until back measures 43(48:54:62)cm/17(19: 21 ¼:24 ½)in from cast on edge, ending with a wrong side row.
Shape back neck
Next row K32(36:40:44), turn and work on these sts.
Dec one st at neck edge on next 4 rows. 28(32:36:40) sts.
Work 1 row.
Shape shoulder
Cast off 7(8:9:10) sts at the beg of next and 2 foll alt rows.
Work 1 row.
Cast off rem 7(8:9:10) sts.
With right side facing slip centre 26(28:30:32) sts on a holder, rejoin yarn to rem sts, k to end.
Dec one st at neck edge on next 4 rows. 28(32:36:40) sts.
Work 2 rows.
Shape shoulder
Cast off 7(8:9:10) sts at the beg of next and 2 foll alt rows.
Work 1 row.
Cast off rem 7(8:9:10) sts.

FRONT

Work as given for back until front measures 40(45:48:56)cm/ 15 ¾(17 ¾:19:22)in from cast on edge, ending with a wrong side row.
Shape front neck
Next row K35(39:43:47), turn and work on these sts.
Dec one st at neck edge on every row until 28(32:36:40) sts rem.
Work straight until front measures the same as back to shoulder, ending at armhole edge.
Shape shoulder
Cast off 7(8:9:10) sts at the beg of next and 2 foll alt rows.
Work 1 row.
Cast off rem 7(8:9:10) sts.
With right side facing, slip centre 20(22:24:26) sts on a holder, rejoin yarn to rem sts, k to end.
Dec one st at neck edge on every row until 28(32:36:40) sts rem.
Work straight until front measures the same as back to shoulder, ending at armhole edge.
Shape shoulder
Cast off 7(8:9:10) sts at the beg of next and 2 foll alt rows.
Work 1 row.
Cast off rem 7(8:9:10) sts.

POCKETS (make 2)

With 3.25mm (US 3) needles and Lilac Blossom cast on 22(24:26:28) sts.
Beg with a k row cont in st st and stripes of 6(6:7:7) rows Lilac Blossom, 4(4:5:5) rows Daisy Yellow, 4(4:5:5) rows Midnight, 6(6:7:7) rows Grass, 4(4:5:5) rows Fuchsia and 6(6:7:7) rows Seaside.
Cast off.

LEFT POCKET EDGING

With right side facing, using 3.25mm (US 3) needles and Midnight, starting at cast off edge, pick up and k22(22:28:28) sts evenly along row ends.
1st row P3, [k4, p2] 2(2:3:3) times, k4, p3.
2nd row K3, [p4, k2] 2(2:3:3) times, p4, k3.
Rep the last 2 rows 3 times more.
Cast off in rib.

RIGHT POCKET EDGING

With right side facing, using 3.25mm (US 3) needles and Midnight, starting at cast on edge, pick up and k22(22:28:28) sts evenly along row ends.
1st row P3, [k4, p2] 2(2:3:3) times, k4, p3.
2nd row K3, [p4, k2] 2(2:3:3) times, p4, k3.
Rep the last 2 rows 3 times more.
Cast off in rib.

NECKBAND

Join right shoulder seam.
With 3.25mm (US 3) needles and Midnight pick up and k20(21:22:23) sts down left side of front neck, k20(22:24:26) sts on front neck holder, pick up and k19(20:21:22) sts up right side of front neck, 6 sts down right side of back neck, k26(28:30:32) sts on back neck holder, pick up and k7 sts up left side of back neck. 98(104:110:116) sts.
1st row P2, [k4, p2] to end.
2nd row K2, [p4, k2] to end.
Rep the last 2 rows 3 times more.
Cast off in rib.

ARMBANDS

Join left shoulder and neckband seam.
With 3mm (US 2) needles and Midnight pick up and k50(56:62:68) sts evenly round armhole edge.
1st row P2, [k4, p2] to end.
2nd row K2, [p4, k2] to end.
Rep the last 2 rows 3 times more.
Cast off in rib.

TO MAKE UP

Join side, sleeve and armband seams. Sew on pockets.

MILLAMIA
HAT AND SCARF

From left to right: **MillaMia Hat and Scarf** in Seaside (161) and Snow (124) patterns on page 74, **MillaMia Hat and Scarf** in Fuchsia (143) and Forget me not (120) patterns on page 74

MILLAMIA HAT & SCARF

SKILL LEVEL Beginner / Improving

SIZES / MEASUREMENTS

To fit age   One size to fit 1-3 years

ACTUAL SCARF MEASUREMENTS

Length	110	cm
	43 ¼	in
Width	15	cm
	6	in

MATERIALS

Hat

- Two 50g/1 ¾oz balls of MillaMia Naturally Soft Merino in Fuchsia (143) (M).
- One ball contrast in Forget me not (120) (C).
- Pair each of 3mm (US 2) and 3.25mm (US 3) knitting needles.

Scarf

- Two 50g/1 ¾oz balls of MillaMia Naturally Soft Merino in Fuchsia (143) (M).
- One ball contrast in Forget me not (120) (C).
- If knitting both the scarf and hat, one ball of contrast colour (C) will be enough for both items.
- Pair of 3.25mm (US 3) knitting needles.

TENSION / GAUGE

25 sts and 34 rows to 10cm/4in over st st using 3.25mm (US 3) needles.

HINTS AND TIPS

Simple shapes to knit with the construction made more interesting and challenging by the addition of the nordic star motif placed either in Fair Isle or Swiss darning. By choosing strongly contrasting colours the star design will really stand out.

ABBREVIATIONS

See page 9.

SUGGESTED ALTERNATIVE COLOURWAYS

Seaside 161   Snow 124   Midnight 101   Petal 122   Storm 102   Lilac Blossom 123

NOTE

When working from Chart, use the Fair Isle method and strand yarn not in use loosely across back of work.

Read odd numbered rows (right side) rows from right to left and even numbered rows from left to right.

Alternatively the hat can be knitted in the background colour and the motif Swiss / duplicate darned when the work is completed.

110 cm
43 ¼ in

15 cm
6 in

HAT

With 3.25mm (US 3) needles and M, cast on 110 sts.
1st row P2, [k4, p2] to end.
2nd row K2, [p4, k2] to end.
These 2 rows form the rib.
Work a further 2 rows C, 10 rows M, 2 rows C, 2 rows M.
Mark each end of last row with a coloured thread to mark fold line for brim.
Cont in M.
Change to 3mm (US 2) needles.
Work a further 17 rows in rib, inc one st at centre of last row. 111 sts.
Change to 3.25mm (US 3) needles.
Starting with a k row cont in st st.
Work 4 rows.
Place motif *
Next row K43M, work across 1st row of Chart, k43M.
Next row P43M, work across 2nd row of Chart, p43M.
Cont in this way to end of Chart.
Cont in M until hat measures 15cm/6in from coloured thread, ending with a p row.

If Swiss/duplicate darning rather than placing motif with Fair Isle knitting, mark this row with some form of row marker to make it easier to find where to position the motif later.

Shape top
1st row [K10, k2 tog] 9 times, k3.
2nd row P to end.
3rd row [K9, k2 tog] 9 times, k3.
4th row P to end.
5th row [K8, k2 tog] 9 times, k3.
6th row P to end.
7th row [K7, k2 tog] 9 times, k3.
8th row P to end.
9th row [K6, k2 tog] 9 times, k3.
10th row P to end.
11th row [K5, k2 tog] 9 times, k3.
12th row P to end.
13th row [K4, k2 tog] 9 times, k3.
14th row P to end.
15th row [K3, k2 tog] 9 times, k3.
16th row P to end.
17th row [K2, k2 tog] 9 times, k3.
18th row P to end.
19th row [K1, k2 tog] 9 times, k3.
20th row P to end.
Next row [K2 tog] 10 times, k1.
Next row [P2 tog] 5 times, p1.
Leaving a long end, cut off yarn and thread through rem sts, pull up and secure.
Join seam, reversing seam for brim.

If you have not placed the motif using the Fair Isle method, you should now Swiss/ duplicate darn the motif on front of hat.

CHART

25

20

15

10

5

1

— 25 st rep —

Key

■ M-Fuchsia (143)
□ C-Forget me not (120)

SCARF

With 3.25mm (US 3) needles and M cast on 39 sts.
K 3 rows.
Next row (right side) K to end.
Next row K3, p to last 3 sts, k3.
These 2 rows form the patt of st st with g-st border.
Work a further 6 rows M, 4 rows C, 8 rows M, 4 rows C,
4 rows M.
Place motif *
Next row K7M, work across 1st row of Chart, k7M.
Next row K3, p4 using M, work across 2nd row of Chart, using
M, p4, k3.
Cont in this way to end of Chart.
Cont in M and patt until scarf measures 94cm/37in from cast
on edge, ending with a wrong side row.
Place motif *
Next row K7M, work across 1st row of Chart, k7M.
Next row K3, p4 using M, work across 2nd row of Chart, using
M, p4, k3.
Cont in this way to end of Chart.
Cont in M and patt, work a further 5 rows M, 4 rows C, 8 rows
M, 4 rows C, 8 rows M.
Using M k 4 rows.
Cast off.

If you have not placed the motif using the Fair Isle method,
you should now Swiss/ duplicate darn the motif to each
end of scarf.

*If Swiss/duplicate darning rather than placing motif with Fair Isle
knitting, mark this row with some form of row marker (e.g. different
coloured thread) to make it easier to find where to position the motif.*

NIKLAS
CARDIGAN

From left to right: **Niklas Cardigan**
in Daisy Yellow (142), Fuchsia (143)
and Putty Grey (121);
Niklas Cardigan in Peacock (144),
Midnight (101) and Putty Grey (121)
pattern on page 80

NIKLAS CARDIGAN

SKILL LEVEL **Beginner / Improving**

SIZES / MEASUREMENTS

To fit age	1-2	2-3	3-4	4-5	years

ACTUAL GARMENT MEASUREMENTS

Chest	58	62	67	72	cm
	23	24 ½	26 ½	28 ¼	in
Length to shoulder	28	32	36	40	cm
	11	12 ½	14 ¼	15 ¾	in
Sleeve length	21	25	27	28	cm
	8 ¼	9 ¾	10 ½	11	in

MATERIALS

- 2(2:2:3) 50g/1 ¾oz balls of MillaMia Naturally Soft Merino in each of Midnight (101) (M) and Putty Grey (121) (A).
- Two balls in Peacock (144) (B).
- Pair each of 3mm (US 2) and 3.25mm (US 3) knitting needles.
- Circular 3mm (US 2) knitting needle.
- 3 buttons approx 18mm/¾in diameter.

GAUGE / TENSION

25 sts and 34 rows to 10cm/4in square over st st using 3.25mm (US 3) needles.

HINTS AND TIPS

Such a rewarding knit, the stripes keep it interesting for you while knitting and the addition of an accent third shade means that you can easily incorporate a child's favourite colour without it dominating the entire garment. As you can see from our photos it can be used for dress down occasions with jeans or as a finishing touch to a party outfit.

ABBREVIATIONS

See page 9.

SUGGESTED ALTERNATIVE COLOURWAYS

Fuchsia	Putty	Daisy	Claret	Fawn	Seaside
143	Grey	Yellow	104	160	161
	121	142			

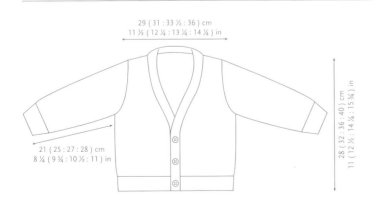

29 (31 : 33 ½ : 36) cm
11 ½ (12 ¼ : 13 ¼ : 14 ¼) in

28 (32 : 36 : 40) cm
11 (12 ½ : 14 ¼ : 15 ¾) in

21 (25 : 27 : 28) cm
8 ¼ (9 ¾ : 10 ½ : 11) in

BACK

With 3mm (US 2) needles and B cast on 74(80:86:92) sts.
1st rib row K2, [p1, k2] to end.
2nd rib row P2, [k1, p2] to end.
Rep the last 2 rows 7 times more.
Cut off B.
Change to 3.25mm (US 3) needles.
Beg with a k row, cont in st st and stripes of 4 rows M and 4 rows A until back measures 16(19:22:25)cm/6 ¼(7 ½:8 ¾: 9 ¾)in from cast on edge, ending with a p row. (Note patt row).
Shape armholes
Cast off 3(3:4:4) sts at beg of next 2 rows. 68(74:78:84) sts.
Next row K2, skpo, k to last 4 sts, k2 tog, k2.
Next row P to end.
Rep the last 2 rows 5(6:6:7) times. 56(60:64:68) sts.
Cont in st st until back measures 28(32:36:40)cm/11(12 ½: 14 ¼:15 ¾)in from cast on edge, ending with a p row.
Shape shoulders
Cast off 6(7:7:8) sts at beg of next 2 rows and 7(7:8:8) sts at beg of foll 2 rows.
Leave rem 30(32:34:36) sts on a holder.

LEFT FRONT

With 3mm (US 2) needles and B cast on 33(36:39:42) sts.
1st rib row [K2, p1] to end.
2nd rib row [K1, p2] to end.
Rep the last 2 rows 7 times more.
Cut off B.
Change to 3.25mm (US 3) needles.
Beg with a k row, cont in st st and stripes of 4 rows M and 4 rows A until 16 rows less than back to armhole shaping have been worked, ending with a p row.
Shape front neck
Next row K to last 4 sts, k2 tog, k2.
Work 3 rows.
Rep the last 4 rows 3 times more.

Shape armhole and front neck
Next row Cast off 3(3:4:4) sts, k to last 4 sts, k2 tog, k2. 25(28:30:33) sts.
Next row P to end.
Next row K2, skpo, k to end.
Next row P to end.
Next row K2, skpo, k to last 4 sts, k2 tog, k2.
Next row P to end.
Rep the last 4 rows 2(2:2:3) times.
2nd and 3rd sizes only
Next row K2, skpo, k to end.
Next row P to end.
All sizes
16(18:20:21) sts.
Keeping armhole edge straight cont to dec at neck edge as set on every 4th row until 13(14:15:16) sts rem.
Work straight until front matches back to shoulder, ending at armhole edge.
Shape shoulder
Cast off 6(7:7:8) sts at beg of next row.
Work 1 row.
Cast off rem 7(7:8:8) sts.

RIGHT FRONT

With 3mm (US 2) needles and B cast on 33(36:39:42) sts.
1st rib row [P1, k2] to end.
2nd rib row [P2, k1] to end.
Rep the last 2 rows 7 times more.
Cut off B.
Change to 3.25mm (US 3) needles.
Beg with a k row, cont in st st and stripes of 4 rows M and 4 rows A until 16 rows less than back to armhole shaping have been worked, ending with a p row.
Shape front neck
Next row K2, skpo, k to end.
Work 3 rows.
Rep the last 4 rows 3 times more.

Shape armhole and front neck

Next row K2, skpo, k to end.

Next row Cast off 3(3:4:4) sts, p to end. 25(28:30:33) sts.

Next row K to last 4 sts, k2 tog, k2.

Next row P to end.

Next row K2, skpo, k to last 4 sts, k2 tog, k2.

Next row P to end.

Rep the last 4 rows 2(2:2:3) times.

2nd and 3rd sizes only

Next row K to last 4 sts, k2 tog, k2.

Next row P to end.

All sizes

16(18:20:21) sts.

Keeping armhole edge straight cont to dec at neck edge as set on every 4th row until 13(14:15:16) sts rem.

Work straight until front matches back to shoulder, ending at armhole edge.

Shape shoulder

Cast off 6(7:7:8) sts at beg of next row.

Work 1 row.

Cast off rem 7(7:8:8) sts.

SLEEVES

With 3mm (US 2) needles and B cast on 41(44:47:53) sts.

1st rib row K2, [p1, k2] to end.

2nd rib row P2, [k1, p2] to end.

Rep the last 2 rows 7 times more.

Cut off B.

Change to 3.25mm (US 3) needles.

Beg with a k row, cont in st st and stripes of 4 rows M, [4 rows A, 4 rows M] 3(4:4:5) times, [4 rows B, 4 rows M] twice, then cont in stripes of 4 rows A, 4 rows M to end **at the same time** work increases as follows:

Work 2 rows.

Inc row K3, m1, k to last 3 sts, m1, k3.

Work 5 rows.

Rep the last 6 rows 6(7:8:8) times more and then the inc row again. 57(62:67:73) sts.

Cont straight until sleeve measures approx 21(25:27:28)cm/ 8 ¼(9 ¾:10 ½:11)in from cast on edge, ending with same patt row as back at underarm.

Shape sleeve top

Cast off 3(3:4:4) sts at beg of next 2 rows. 51(56:59:65) sts.

Next row K2, skpo, k to last 4 sts, k2 tog, k2.

Next row P to end.

Rep the last 2 rows 5(6:6:7) times. 39(42:45:49) sts.

Cast off 3 sts at beg of next 8(8:10:12) rows.

Cast off.

FRONT BAND

Join shoulder seams.

With right side facing, 3mm (US 2) circular needle and B, pick up and k32(40:48:56) sts up right front edge, to beg of neck shaping, 41(44:47:50) sts along right front neck edge, 30(32:34:36) sts from back neck, pick up and k41(44:47:50) sts down left front neck edge to beg of neck shaping, 32(40:48:56) sts along left front edge. 176(200:224:248) sts.

1st rib row P2, [k1, p2] to end.

2nd rib row K2, [p1, k2] to end.

Rib 2 more rows.

Girl's version

Buttonhole row Rib 144(162:180:198), [p2 tog, y2rn, skpo, rib 8(11:14:17)] twice, p2 tog, y2rn, skpo, rib 4.

Boy's version

Buttonhole row Rib 4, [p2 tog, y2rn, skpo, rib 8(11:14:17)] twice, p2 tog, y2rn, skpo, rib to end.

Both versions

Rib 4 more rows working rib 1, rib 1 tbl into y2rn on 1st row.

Cast off in rib.

TO MAKE UP

Join side and sleeve seams. Sew in sleeves. Sew on buttons.

From left to right: **Oskar Jumper**
in Midnight (101), Snow (124),
Claret (104), Plum (162),
Seaside (161) and Peacock (144)
pattern on page 88,
Rafael Top in Midnight (101),
Snow (124), Plum (162),
Claret (104), Fuchsia (143),
Grass (141), Forget me not (120)
and Daisy Yellow (142)
pattern on page 92

OSKAR
JUMPER
RAFAEL
TOP

OSKAR JUMPER

SKILL LEVEL Experienced

SIZES / MEASUREMENTS

To fit age	1-2	2-3	3-4	4-5	years

ACTUAL GARMENT MEASUREMENTS

Chest	53	58	62	67	cm
	21	23	24 ½	26 ½	in
Length to	28	32	36	40	cm
shoulder	11	12 ½	14 ¼	15 ¾	in
Sleeve	21	24	26	28	cm
length	8 ¼	9 ½	10 ¼	11	in

MATERIALS

- Two 50g/1 ¾oz balls of MillaMia Naturally Soft Merino in each of Midnight (101) (M) and Snow (124) (A).
- One ball in each of Seaside (161) (B), Claret (104) (C), Plum (162) (D) and Peacock (144) (E).
- Pair each of 3mm (US 2) and 3.25mm (US 3) knitting needles.

TENSION / GAUGE

25 sts and 34 rows to 10cm/4in square over st st using 3.25mm (US 3) needles.

HINTS AND TIPS

This retro inspired jumper looks gorgeous when styled with jeans. By choosing softer lighter colours it is equally suitable for a little girl. Make a conscious effort not to pull the yarn you are carrying behind the piece too tight when working in Fair Isle as you do not want to cause the body to pucker.

ABBREVIATIONS

See page 9.

SUGGESTED ALTERNATIVE COLOURWAY

Plum	Snow	Seaside	Midnight	Petal	Fuchsia
162	124	161	101	122	143

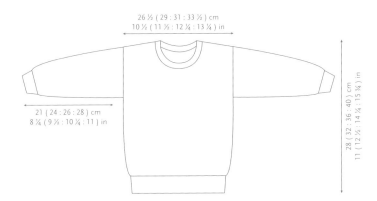

26 ½ (29 : 31 : 33 ½) cm
10 ½ (11 ½ : 12 ¼ : 13 ¼) in

21 (24 : 26 : 28) cm
8 ¼ (9 ½ : 10 ¼ : 11) in

28 (32 : 36 : 40) cm
11 (12 ½ : 14 ¼ : 15 ¾) in

BACK

With 3mm (US 2) needles and M cast on 66(74:78:86) sts.

1st rib row K2, [p2, k2] to end.

2nd rib row P2, [k2, p2] to end.

Rep the last 2 rows 7 times more and then the 1st row again.

Inc row Rib to end inc 2(0:2:0) sts evenly across last row.
68(74:80:86) sts.

Change to 3.25mm (US 3) needles.

Beg with a k row, cont in st st.

Work 2 rows M and 1 row E.

Work in patt from Chart A, beg with a p row.

Work 1 row E, 1 row C.

Work in patt from Chart B, ending with a k row.

Work 1 row C, 2 rows B, 1 row C.

Now work from Chart C to end, beg with a p row.

Cont in patt until back measures 26(30:34:38)cm/10 ¼
(11 ¾:13 ½:15)in from cast on edge, ending with a p row.

Shape back neck

Next row Patt 23(25:27:29) sts, turn and work on these sts.

Dec one st at neck edge on next 4 rows. 19(21:23:25) sts.

Work 1 row.

Shape shoulder

Cast off 6(7:8:9) sts at the beg of next and foll alt row.

Work 1 row.

Cast off rem 7 sts.

With right side facing, slip centre 22(24:26:28) sts on a holder,
rejoin yarn to rem sts, patt to end.

Dec one st at neck edge on next 4 rows. 19(21:23:25) sts.

Work 2 rows.

Shape shoulder

Cast off 6(7:8:9) sts at the beg of next and foll alt row.

Work 1 row.

Cast off rem 7 sts.

CHART A

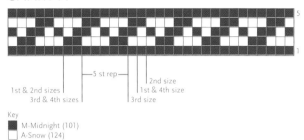

Key
■ M-Midnight (101)
☐ A-Snow (124)

CHART B

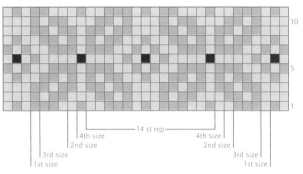

Key
 B-Seaside (161)
■ C-Claret (104)
▨ D-Plum (162)

CHART C

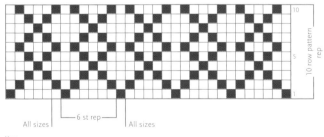

Key
■ M-Midnight (101)
☐ A-Snow (124)

FRONT

Work as given for back until front measures 23(27:31:35)cm/
9(10 ½:12 ¼:13 ¾)in from cast on edge, ending
with a p row.

Shape front neck

Next row Patt 28(30:32:34), turn and work on these sts.
Dec one st at neck edge on next and 8 foll rows.
19(21:23:25) sts.
Work straight until front measures same as back to shoulder,
ending at armhole edge.

Shape shoulder

Cast off 6(7:8:9) sts at the beg of next and foll alt row.
Work 1 row.
Cast off rem 7 sts.
With right side facing, slip centre 12(14:16:18) sts on a holder,
rejoin yarn to rem sts, patt to end.
Dec one st at neck edge on next and 8 foll rows.
19(21:23:25) sts.
Work straight until front measures same as back to shoulder,
ending at armhole edge.

Shape shoulder

Cast off 6(7:8:9) sts at the beg of next and foll alt row.
Work 1 row.
Cast off rem 7 sts.

LEFT SLEEVE

With 3mm (US 2) needles and M cast on 42(42:46:50) sts.
1st rib row K2, [p2, k2] to end.
2nd rib row P2, [k2, p2] to end.
These 2 rows form the rib.
Work a further 2 rows E, 2 rows M, 1 row E.
Next row Using E rib to end dec(inc:inc:inc) 1(2:1:4) sts evenly
across row. 41(44:47:54) sts.
Cut off E.

Change to 3.25mm (US 3) needles.
Beg with a k row, cont in st st and M only.
Work 2 rows.
Inc row K3, m1, k to last 3 sts, m1, k3.
Work 5 rows.
Rep the last 6 rows 6(7:8:9) times more and then the inc row
again. 57(62:67:76) sts.
Cont straight until sleeve measures 21(24:26:28)cm/8 ¼
(9 ½:10 ¼:11)in from cast on edge, ending with a p row.
Cast off.

RIGHT SLEEVE

Work as given for left sleeve, using A instead of E.

NECKBAND

Join right shoulder seam.
With 3mm (US 2) needles and M pick up and k21 sts down left
side of front neck, k12(14:16:18) sts on front neck holder, pick
up and k21 sts up right side of front neck, 9 sts down right
side of back neck, k22(24:26:28) sts on back neck holder, pick
up and k9 sts up left side of back neck. 94(98:102:106) sts.
1st row K2, [p2, k2] to end.
2nd row P2, [k2, p2] to end.
Rep the last 2 rows twice more and the 1st row again.
Cast off in rib.

TO MAKE UP

Join left shoulder and neckband. Join side and sleeve seams.
Sew in sleeves.

RAFAEL STRIPED TOP

SKILL LEVEL **Improving**

SIZES / MEASUREMENTS

To fit age	0-3	3-6	6-12	12-18	18-24	mths

ACTUAL GARMENT MEASUREMENTS

Chest	45	51	58	64	70	cm
	17 ½	20	23	25	27 ½	in
Length to	23	26	29	33	38	cm
shoulder	9	10 ¼	11 ½	13	15	in
Sleeve	13	15	16	18	20	cm
length	5 ¼	6	6 ¼	7	8	in

MATERIALS

- 1(1:1:2:2) 50g/1 ¾oz balls of MillaMia Naturally Soft Merino in Midnight (101) (A).
- One ball in each of Snow (124) (B), Plum (162) (C), Claret (104) (D), Fuchsia (143) (E), Grass (141) (F), Forget me not (120) (G) and Daisy Yellow (142) (H).
- Pair each of 3mm (US 2) and 3.25mm (US 3) knitting needles.

TENSION / GAUGE

25 sts and 34 rows to 10cm/4in square over st st using 3.25mm (US 3) needles.

HINTS AND TIPS

You can avoid cutting the yarn so many times on this striped top by working with double pointed needles or a short circular needle instead. Remembering that stocking stitch is produced by knitting on the right side and purling on the wrong side, you can choose to work several rows on the right/wrong side consecutively as opposed to alternating as you would normally, by sliding the stitches back along the needle.

Alternatively you could work the main body on circular needles in the round (as opposed to back and forth) to avoid cutting the yarn. Simply cast on twice the number of required stitches for the front, marking the first stitch and halfway stitch with a coloured thread, and then work in the round carrying the various colours up the inside of the top until they are used again. Split the work at markers between a holder and a pair of straight knitting needles once you reach the 'Shape neck' instructions and continue working back and forth instead of in the round. Consider making also the Bo Bonnet in matching colours to use up any leftover yarn.

ABBREVIATIONS

See page 9.

SUGGESTED ALTERNATIVE COLOURWAY

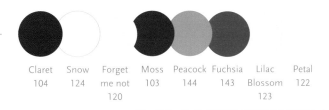

Claret	Snow	Forget	Moss	Peacock	Fuchsia	Lilac	Petal
104	124	me not	103	144	143	Blossom	122
		120				123	

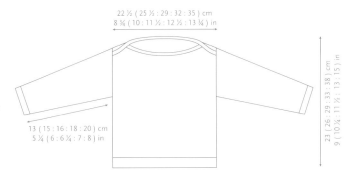

22 ½ (25 ½ : 29 : 32 : 35) cm
8 ¾ (10 : 11 ½ : 12 ½ : 13 ¾) in

13 (15 : 16 : 18 : 20) cm
5 ¼ (6 : 6 ¼ : 7 : 8) in

23 (26 : 29 : 33 : 38) cm
9 (10 ¼ : 11 ½ : 13 : 15) in

STRIPE SEQUENCE

0(2:2:2:4) rows B, [2 rows A, 1 row B] 0(2:4:6:8) times, 0(2:2:2:2) rows A, 2(4:4:4:4) rows B, 2 rows A, 1 row B, 2 rows A, 1 row D, [2 rows A, 2 rows C] 2(2:3:4:5) times, [2 rows D, 2 rows B] 1(1:1:2:3) times, 2 rows D, 1 row C, 1 row B, 1 row C, 1 row H, 1 row C, 2 rows D, 2 rows G, 1 row D, 1 row A, 1 row D, 2 rows G, 2 rows D, 1 row B, 1 row D, [1 row A, 1 row C] twice, 1 row A, 1 row D, 2 rows G, 1 row F, 1 row E, 1 row F, 1 row A, 1 row F, 1 row H, 2 rows G, 1 row A, 2 rows G, 1 row E, 2 rows A, [2 rows G, 1 row D] twice, 1 row B, 1 row F, 1 row H, 1 row G, 1 row A, 1 row G, 2 rows C, 2 rows G.
78(90:100:114:130) rows.

BACK and FRONT (both alike)

With 3.25mm (US 3) needles and A, cast on 58(66:74:82:90) sts.
1st rib row K2, * p2, k2; rep from * to end.
2nd rib row P2, * k2, p2; rep from * to end.
Rep the last 2 rows twice more.
Beg with a k row, cont in st st and stripes until 68(78:86:98:112) rows have been worked.
Shape neck
Next row (right side) K16(19:22:25:28), turn and work on these sts for first side of neck shaping.
Next row Cast off 3 sts, p to end.
Next row K to end.
Rep the last 2 rows 0(1:2:3:4) times more. 13 sts.
Mark beg of last row with a coloured thread.
Next row P2 tog, p to end.
Next row K to last 2 sts, k2 tog.
Rep the last 2 rows twice more and the 1st row again. 6 sts.
Leave these sts on a holder.
With right side facing, place centre 26(28:30:32:34) sts on a holder, rejoin yarn to rem sts, k to end.
Next row P to end.
Next row Cast off 3 sts, k to end.
Rep the last 2 rows 0(1:2:3:4) times more. 13 sts.

Mark end of last row with a coloured thread.
Next row P to last 2 sts, p2 tog tbl.
Next row K2 tog tbl, k to end.
Rep the last 2 rows twice more and the 1st row again. 6 sts.
Leave these sts on a holder.
Neck Edging
With right side facing using using 3mm (US 2) needles and D, k6 sts from holder, pick up and k13(16:19:20:23) sts around shaped edge, k across centre 26(28:30:32:34) sts, pick up and k13(16:19:20:23) sts around shaped edge, k6 from holder.
64(72:80:84:92) sts.
K 3 rows.
Cast off.

SLEEVES

Using 3.25mm (US 3) needles and A, cast on 34(34:38:38:42) sts.
1st rib row K2, * p2, k2; rep from * to end.
2nd rib row P2, * k2, p2; rep from * to end.
Rep the last 2 rows once more, inc 2(4:2:4:2) sts evenly across last row. 36(38:40:42:44) sts.
Beg with a k row, cont in st st, and stripes **at the same time** inc (2 sts from side seam) one st at each end of every 3rd row until there are 48(54:60:68:74) sts.
Cont straight until sleeve measures 13(15:16:18:20)cm/5 ¼ (6:6 ¼:7:8)in from cast on edge, ending with a wrong side row.
Cast off.

MAKE UP

Matching coloured threads on shoulder, lap front over back and tack to form envelope neck. Sew on sleeves, placing centre of sleeves to coloured threads. Join side and sleeve seams.

BO BONNET

SKILL LEVEL **Beginner / Improving**

SIZES / MEASUREMENTS
To fit age 6-24   24-60   mths

MATERIALS
• 1(2) 50g/1 ¾oz balls of MillaMia Naturally Soft Merino in Claret (104) (D).
• Small amounts in each of Midnight (101) (A), Snow (124) (B), Plum (162) (C), Fuchsia (143) (E), Grass (141) (F), Forget me not (120) (G) and Daisy Yellow (142) (H). There will be sufficient yarn over from Rafael Striped Top for these small amounts.
• Pair each of 3mm (US 2) and 3.25mm (US 3) knitting needles.
• One button approx 21mm/⅞in diameter.

TENSION / GAUGE
25 sts and 34 rows to 10cm/4in square over st st using 3.25mm (US 3) needles.

HINTS AND TIPS
Echo a bygone era with this beautiful bonnet. It teams perfectly with the Rafael Striped Top and is a great way to use up leftover yarn if you have knitted Rafael.

ABBREVIATIONS
See page 9.

SUGGESTED ALTERNATIVE COLOURWAY

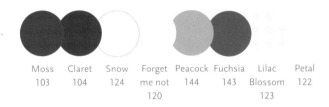

Moss	Claret	Snow	Forget me not	Peacock	Fuchsia	Lilac Blossom	Petal
103	104	124	120	144	143	123	122

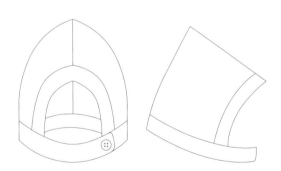

TO MAKE

Using 3.25mm (US 3) needles and D, cast on 76(88) sts.
Beg with a k row cont in st st until work measures 14(17)cm/
5 ½(6 ¾)in, ending with a p row.

Shape top

Next row K35(41), k2 tog, k2, skpo, k to end.
Next row P to end.
Next row K34(40), k2 tog, k2, skpo, k to end.
Next row P to end.
Next row K33(39), k2 tog, k2, skpo, k to end.
Next row P to end.
Next row K32(38), k2 tog, k2, skpo, k to end.
Next row P to end. 68(80) sts.
Next row K34(40), turn and work on these sts.
Next row Cast off 6 sts, p to end.
Next row K to end.
Rep the last 2 rows 3(4) times more.
Cast off rem 10 sts.
With right side facing, rejoin yarn to rem sts.
Next row Cast off 6 sts, k to end.
Next row P to end.
Rep the last 2 rows 3(4) times more.
Cast off rem 10 sts.

Face edging

Join top seam.
Using 3mm (US 2) needles and A, with right side facing pick
up and k104(128) sts round face edge.
K 1 row A, 4 rows G, 2 rows H, 2 rows E, 4 rows B, 4 rows C,
2 rows F, 1 row A.
Using A cast off.

Neck edging

Using 3mm (US 2) needles and A, with right side facing pick
up and k7 sts across row ends of left face edging, 66(78) sts
round neck edge, pick up and k7 sts across row ends of right
face edging, then cast on 20 sts. 100(112) sts.
K 1 row A, 4 rows G, 2 rows H, 1 row E.
1st buttonhole row Using E, k5, k2 tog, y2rn, skpo, k to end.
2nd buttonhole row Using B, k to end, working k1, k1 tbl
into y2rn.
K 3 rows B, 4 rows C, 2 rows F, 1 row A.
Using A cast off.

To complete

Sew on button.

PERNILLA
DRESS

From left to right: **Pernilla Dress** in Fuchsia (143), **Pernilla Dress** in Peacock (144) and **Pernilla Dress** in Grass (141) pattern on page 102

PERNILLA DRESS

SKILL LEVEL **Beginner / Improving**

SIZES / MEASUREMENTS

To fit age	1-2	2-3	3-4	4-5	years

ACTUAL GARMENT MEASUREMENTS

Chest	58	63	68	73	cm
	23	24 ¾	26 ¾	28 ¾	in
Length to	45	50	56	64	cm
shoulder	17 ¾	19 ¾	22	25 ¼	in

MATERIALS

- 5(6:6:7) 50g/1 ¾oz balls of MillaMia Naturally Soft Merino in Grass (141).
- Pair each of 3mm (US 2) and 3.25mm (US 3) knitting needles.
- 135cm/53in grosgrain ribbon (approx 30mm/1 ¼in wide).

GAUGE / TENSION

25 sts and 34 rows to 10cm/4in square over st st using 3.25mm(US 3) needles.

HINTS AND TIPS

We teamed this dress with a navy and white grosgrain ribbon, as we felt this worked well with all colourways. Play around and try also a matching (or contrast) colour satin ribbon to give the finished dress a different look. Take some time to place the ribbon loops to make sure that they sit evenly and neatly on the dress. This makes all the difference to the finished impact of the item. Consider folding the ends of the ribbon over twice and then sewing them to stop the ribbon fraying if using grosgrain.

ABBREVIATIONS

See page 9.

SUGGESTED ALTERNATIVE COLOURWAYS

Fuchsia	Peacock	Plum	Midnight	Petal
143	144	162	101	122

29 (31 ½ : 34 : 36 ½) cm
11 ½ (12 ½ : 13 ½ : 14 ½) in

45 (50 : 56 : 64) cm
17 ¾ (19 ¾ : 22 : 25 ¼) in

BACK

With 3.25mm (US 3) needles cast on 99(111:123:135) sts.
1st row K1, [p1, k1] to end.
Rep the last row 9 times.
Beg with a k row cont in st st.
Work 2(2:6:6) rows.
Dec row K4, skpo, k to last 6 sts, k2 tog, k4.
Work 7(7:5:5) rows.
Rep the last 8(8:6:6) rows 10(13:16:19) times more and then
the dec row again. 75(81:87:93) sts.
Work straight until back measures 34(38:43:50)cm/
13 ½(15:17:19 ¾)in from cast on edge, ending with a wrong
side row.
Shape armholes
Cast off 4(5:6:7) sts at beg of next 2 rows. 67(71:75:79) sts.
Next row K2, skpo, k to last 4 sts, k2 tog, k2.
Next row P to end.
Rep the last 2 rows 6 times more. 53(57:61:65) sts. **
Work 2(6:10:14) rows.
Next row K2, m1, k to last 2 sts, m1, k2.
Next row P to end.
Rep the last 2 rows 6 times more. 67(71:75:79) sts.
Shape back neck
Next row K22(23:24:25), turn and work on these sts.
Dec one st at neck edge on next 4 rows. 18(19:20:21) sts.
Work 1 row.
Shape shoulder
Cast off 6 sts at the beg of next and foll alt row.
Work 1 row.
Cast off rem 6(7:8:9) sts.
With right side facing, slip centre 23(25:27:29) sts on a holder,
rejoin yarn to rem sts, k to end.
Dec one st at neck edge on next 4 rows. 18(19:20:21) sts.
Work 2 rows.

Shape shoulder
Cast off 6 sts at the beg of next and foll alt row.
Work 1 row.
Cast off rem 6(7:8:9) sts.

FRONT

Work as given for back to **. 53(57:61:65) sts.
Work 0(4:8:12) rows.
Shape front neck
Next row K18(19:20:21), turn and work on these sts.
Next row P to end.
Next row K2, m1, k to last 4 sts, k2 tog, k2.
Next row P to end.
Rep the last 2 rows 6 times more. 18(19:20:21) sts.
Work 6 rows.
Shape shoulder
Cast off 6 sts at the beg of next and foll alt row.
Work 1 row.
Cast off rem 6(7:8:9) sts.
With right side facing slip centre 17(19:21:23) sts on a holder,
rejoin yarn to rem sts, k to end.
Next row P to end.
Next row K2, skpo, k to last 2 sts, m1, k2.
Rep the last 2 rows 6 times more. 18(19:20:21) sts.
Work 6 rows.
Shape shoulder
Cast off 6 sts at the beg of next and foll alt row.
Work 1 row.
Cast off rem 6(7:8:9) sts.

NECKBAND

Join right shoulder seam.
With 3mm (US 2) needles pick up and k20 sts down left side of front neck, k17(19:21:23) sts on front neck holder, pick up and k19 sts up right side of front neck, 7 sts down right side of back neck, k23(25:27:29) sts on back neck holder, pick up and k7 sts up left side of back neck. 93(97:101:105) sts.
1st row K1, [p1, k1] to end.
Rep the last row 5 times.
Cast off in moss st.

ARMBANDS

Join left shoulder and neckband seam.
With 3mm (US 2) needles pick up and k61(67:73:79) sts evenly round armhole edge.
1st row K1, [p1, k1] to end.
Rep the last row 3 times.
Cast off in moss st.

RIBBON LOOPS (make 4)

With 3mm (US 2) needles cast on 9 sts.
1st row K1, [p1, k1] to end.
Rep the last row 2 times.
Cast off in moss st.

TO MAKE UP

Join side and armband seams. Sew on ribbon loops, 2 on front and 2 on back. Thread ribbon through loops to tie at front.

YARN COLOURS

Midnight
101

Storm
102

Moss
103

Claret
104

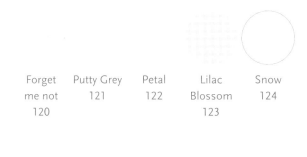

Forget
me not
120

Putty Grey
121

Petal
122

Lilac
Blossom
123

Snow
124

Scarlet
140

Grass
141

Daisy
Yellow
142

Fuchsia
143

Peacock
144

Fawn
160

Seaside
161

Plum
162

NOTES

INDEX

FELICIA CARDIGAN
page 56

FABIAN TOP
page 62

CARLOTA DRESS
page 66

MILLAMIA HAT & SCARF
page 74

NIKLAS CARDIGAN
page 80

OSKAR JUMPER
page 88

RAFAEL STRIPED TOP
page 92

BO BONNET
page 96

PERNILLA DRESS
page 102

ABOUT MILLAMIA

We started MillaMia in early 2009. As sisters we had long wanted to work together and when we realised that we felt there was a gap in the market for truly stylish, modern baby and children's knitting patterns we decided that this was the ideal opportunity.

Although we both now live in London, England we are originally from Sweden. And our Swedish heritage is very important to us. We have lived all over the world as we were growing up and the one constant we had was spending time every summer in Sweden. Eight weeks a year in the countryside of Sweden, meant plenty of time to learn traditional crafts such as knitting to pass the time.

The MillaMia style is based on the distinctive Swedish aesthetic – clean and contemporary yet with a fun, bright edge. We feel these are qualities ideally suited to children's and baby wear.

As we were disappointed by the range of knitting patterns on offer for babies and children in the market today, we wanted to make sure that our product addressed what we were missing. So in all our designs we have sought to create patterns that have a real design edge but are still fun to knit and practical to use. It is really important to us that each of our designs are items that we would actually like to dress our kids, nieces and nephews in.

Luckily Helena has a background in fashion design. Her experience has ranged from adult clothing to accessories and textiles. As such her designs for MillaMia are not constrained by conventional knitting or what has gone before. She applies the same techniques to designing a MillaMia collection that she uses for fashion design – taking account of current trends while at the same time directing our collections to produce clothes that you will want to keep for years. This has resulted in our patterns, imagery and use of colour being quite different from what is already available today.

The Bright Young Things collection, in particular, reflects our love of colour. Our yarn colours have been designed from first principles resulting in a palette that is unique to our brand and that make our designs stand out from the crowd. We get so excited when we see our yarns being put together in new combinations of colour. It demonstrates to us how important a part colour plays in design, and reminds us of why we love knitting. Simply playing with colours is a wonderful way to engage in the design process, and this is what knitting allows.

The MillaMia offering is based around our baby and children's knitting patterns and soft Merino yarn. Longer term we hope to take advantage of Helena's bag design skills and introduce really beautiful, contemporary knitting bags, but we are taking it one step at a time. For now we are concentrating on making our core products as good as possible. To help us with this we would really love to hear from our customers. If you have any feedback on MillaMia products, please do get in touch. This is our chance to understand more about what you like and don't like, so that we can improve and enhance our collections. Also do let us know if there is something you would love us to include in our next collections.

With best wishes,

Katarina and Helena Rosén
katarina@millamia.com or helena@millamia.com